THE COMPLETE GUIDE TO
SPORTS

DENNIS PERNU

Sandy Creek
NEW YORK

Sandy Creek
NEW YORK

An Imprint of Sterling Publishing
1166 Avenue of The Americas
New York, NY, 10036

Text © 2015 by QEB Publishing, Inc.
Illustrations © 2015 by QEB Publishing, Inc.

This 2015 edition published by Sandy Creek.

Editorial: Clare Hibbert @ Hollow Pond
Design: Amy McSimpson @ Hollow Pond

ISBN 978-1-4351-6166-5

Manufactured in China
Lot #:
2 4 6 8 10 9 7 5 3
11/15

CONTENTS

Words in **bold** are explained in the Glossary on page 138.

BASEBALL

Baseball is the USA's national sport. Every summer fans flock to ballparks to watch their favorite Major League Baseball (MLB) teams, also called clubs. And many more play baseball for fun and competition. Much like the United States itself, baseball's past is filled with heroes, amazing feats, and even bravery and scandals. No sport is as beloved by Americans. And that love for baseball is spreading around the world!

In the past 25 years many beautiful new ballparks have been built for Major League teams. This is the New York Yankees' ballpark. It can hold more than 49,000 fans for a game.

WOW!

There are 30 teams in Major League Baseball. Every season each team plays 162 regular-season games.

BASEBALL HISTORY

In the 1850s, people began calling baseball America's "national pastime." The United States was a young nation and many people felt it needed a sport to call its own. Much later, some even declared that an American war hero had invented baseball. But the truth was much more complicated.

Mythical Beginnings

Abner Doubleday was an army officer who served in the American Civil War (1861–1865). In 1907 a group of men claimed Doubleday as the official inventor of baseball. The first game, they said, was played in 1839 in Cooperstown, New York. But in 1839, Doubleday lived more than 150 miles from Cooperstown. When Doubleday died he left no proof he had invented baseball.

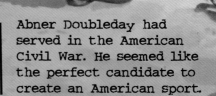

Abner Doubleday had served in the American Civil War. He seemed like the perfect candidate to create an American sport.

This illustration from the 1880s shows an early game of baseball. Thanks to Alexander Cartwright, the field has taken on the diamond shape we recognize today.

Rounders

Today, most agree that baseball grew from **rounders**, an English sport. Baseball and rounders have much in common. Both are played with a hard ball and bat. Both have four **bases**. In 1845 Alexander Cartwright helped modify the rules of rounders. He also introduced the diamond-shaped field. In 1953, Cartwright was finally declared the inventor of the modern game.

Alexander Cartwright was eventually credited for baseball's early rules. Today he is called "the father of baseball."

WOW!

Before Alexander Cartwright's rules, it was legal to put out an opposing player by hitting him with the ball. Ouch!

TAKE ME OUT TO THE BALL GAME

7 LEFTFIELD

6 SHORT STOP

UMPIRE

5 THIRD BASE

BASE COACH

Parts of a Ballpark

A ballpark has an **infield** and an **outfield**. In the infield, three bases, or bags, and **home plate** are arranged in a diamond pattern. The pitcher's mound in the middle of the diamond is 10 inches tall. There are 90 feet between each base and 60.5 feet from the middle of the pitcher's mound to home plate. The large outfield sits past the infield.

There are nine defensive positions on a baseball field (numbered above). This photo also shows the umpires, base coaches, and the batter at home plate.

The pitcher begins a pitch with at least one foot on the white rubber strip located atop the mound. He or she can push off of the rubber with one foot while throwing toward home plate.

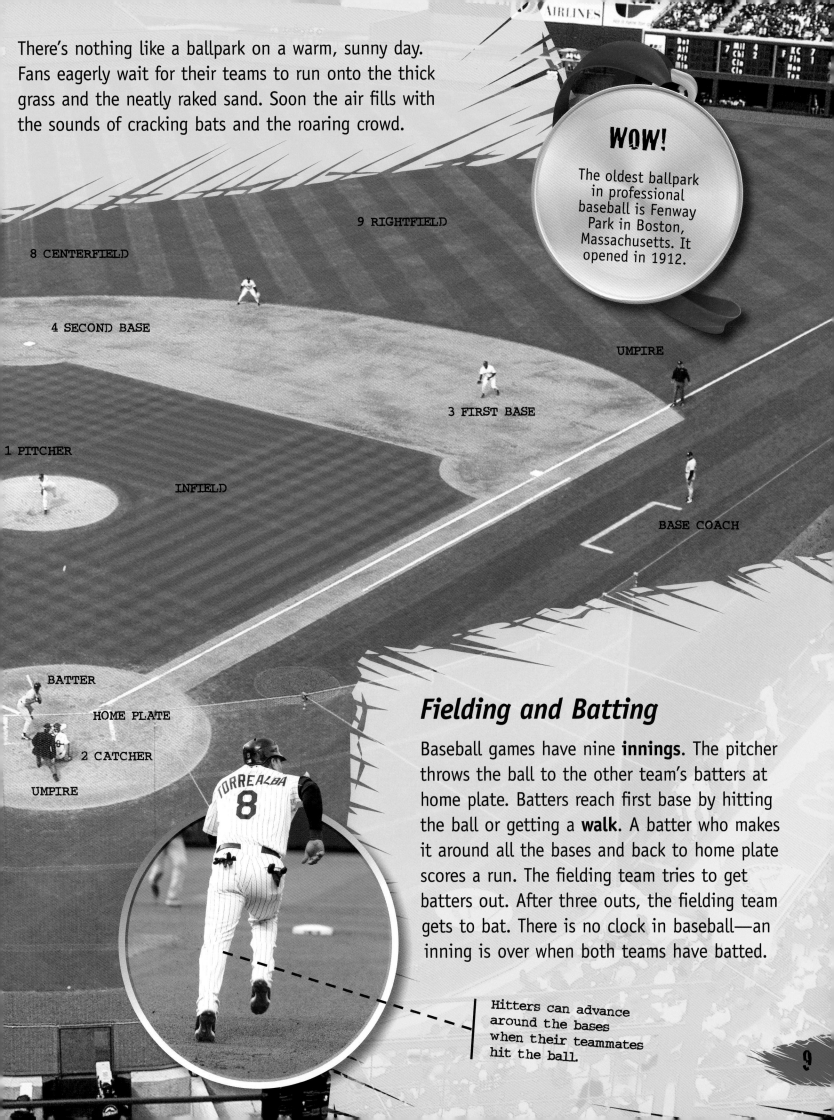

There's nothing like a ballpark on a warm, sunny day. Fans eagerly wait for their teams to run onto the thick grass and the neatly raked sand. Soon the air fills with the sounds of cracking bats and the roaring crowd.

WOW!

The oldest ballpark in professional baseball is Fenway Park in Boston, Massachusetts. It opened in 1912.

9 RIGHTFIELD

8 CENTERFIELD

4 SECOND BASE

UMPIRE

3 FIRST BASE

1 PITCHER

INFIELD

BASE COACH

BATTER

HOME PLATE

2 CATCHER

UMPIRE

TORREALBA 8

Fielding and Batting

Baseball games have nine **innings**. The pitcher throws the ball to the other team's batters at home plate. Batters reach first base by hitting the ball or getting a **walk**. A batter who makes it around all the bases and back to home plate scores a run. The fielding team tries to get batters out. After three outs, the fielding team gets to bat. There is no clock in baseball—an inning is over when both teams have batted.

Hitters can advance around the bases when their teammates hit the ball.

BASEBALL EQUIPMENT

Baseball features less equipment than football, hockey, and many other **contact sports**. You can learn the basics of baseball with just three things: a ball, a bat, and a glove. However, the most popular piece of baseball equipment just might be the cap. You don't have to have one, but it will look great and its visor will help keep the sun out of your eyes!

WOW!

The yarn inside a baseball measures more than 1,100 feet in length.

A baseball glove becomes more comfortable, or "broken in," the more you use it.

Baseball Essentials

A baseball weighs about 5 ounces and has a rubber-coated cork center (the "pill"), wrapped in yarn. Most bats are made of hardwoods such as ash, but some are made of aluminum. Bats range from 24 to 36 inches. Finally, a baseball glove protects your hand when you catch the ball.

More Gear

A baseball is hard and can travel fast, so it's a good idea to wear a helmet when you're at bat. Batting helmets are the rule in all baseball leagues. Some helmets have guards to protect the face. Many players also wear special spiked shoes called cleats. These help players grip the ground when they run.

Batting helmets are made of hard plastic and have soft foam inside of them.

Wooden bats are the rule in pro baseball. Many batters at all levels also wear batting gloves for a better grip.

THE PITCHER

A baseball club has nine players on the field. The focus, however, is usually on the pitcher. He's the only player guaranteed to touch the ball every play.

Man on the Mound

The pitcher tries to throw, or pitch, the ball past the opposing club's batters. Most pitchers can throw different kinds of pitches. A fastball blazes over the plate. A curveball is slower, but it bends as it crosses the plate. If the batter misses the ball, it's a **strike**. After three strikes, the pitcher earns a strikeout.

The strike zone is as wide as the plate and from the batter's knees to armpits. If the pitcher throws the ball here and the batter doesn't swing, it's still a strike.

A pitcher throws the baseball to home plate.

Pitching In

A starting pitcher begins the game. If he gives up too many hits or gets tired, a reliever replaces him. If the reliever helps his team win, he earns a **save**. Some pitchers throw with their left hand, others with their right. "Lefties" have more success against batters who stand on the left side of home plate, and vice versa.

Relievers warm up in the bull pen and wait to be called into the game.

STAR PROFILE
MARIANO RIVERA

Born: November 29, 1969 Panama City, Panama

Team: New York Yankees

Star Stats: 652 saves (MLB record), 5x World Series champion

Pitcher Perfect

Pitchers are under a lot of pressure. But they've also been some of baseball's biggest heroes. Bob Gibson threw 17 strikeouts in Game 1 of the 1968 World Series —still a record. Nolan Ryan pitched for 27 years, throwing 7 **no-hitters**, another MLB record.

WOW!

Cy Young won 511 games from 1890 to 1911.

The Cy Young Award honors Cy Young, pictured here. It is awarded to the best pitcher in each of the MLB's American and National Leagues.

THE BATTER

Hitting a baseball is one of the most difficult feats in all of sports. Some pro pitchers throw the ball nearly 100 miles per hour. It can take just a half-second for the ball to reach the plate. Top hitters need excellent reflexes.

In the Box

The batter faces the pitcher from a **batter's box**. If the batter hits a pitch and reaches first base without getting out, it's a single. Reaching second base is a double, and third base is a triple. If the batter hits the ball over the outfield fence, it's a home run, or "homer." The batter circles all of the bases and scores a run. Any teammates who are on base score too.

STAR PROFILE
BARRY BONDS

Born: July 24, 1964
Riverside, California

Teams: Pittsburgh Pirates, San Francisco Giants

Star Stats: 762 career home runs, 73 home runs in a season (both MLB records)

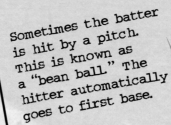

Sometimes the batter is hit by a pitch. This is known as a "bean ball." The hitter automatically goes to first base.

WOW!

Babe Ruth's record of 60 home runs in a season (1927) lasted until 1961.

Super Sluggers

Babe Ruth is one of baseball's biggest legends. He played from 1914 to 1935. Ruth held the record for most career home runs until Hank Aaron passed him in 1973. Then Aaron's record 61 home runs in a season was broken by Mark McGwire in 1998. Barry Bonds later broke both Aaron's and McGwire's records. Ted Williams was another expert hitter. In 1941 his **batting average** was .406. Williams is the last player to finish a season over .400.

In the MLB's American League, teams have a designated hitter. He bats in place of his team's pitcher.

When a batter hits the ball and a teammate on base scores, it's called a run batted in (RBI). Babe Ruth (pictured) had 2,213 career RBIs.

15

THE CATCHER

The pitcher has an important partner. It's the catcher—that player crouching behind home plate. The catcher has many duties. He also needs some special gear to do his job.

Signals and Gear

Catching pitches is not the catcher's only task. He uses secret hand signals to tell the pitcher what pitches to throw. He knows which pitches each batter has problems hitting. And he tries to throw out base runners trying to **steal**. He also wears extra equipment: shin guards, a chest protector, a mask, and a helmet. A special mitt gives the pitcher a target—and the catcher extra padding for his hand.

WOW!
Famed catcher Johnny Bench was named an All-Star 14 times in 17 seasons (1967–1983).

When an opposing base runner tries to steal a base, it's the catcher's job to try to throw him out.

16

Plate Greats

One of the greatest catchers was Yogi Berra. He played 19 years (1946–1965) and was also a good batter. But he was most famous for his crazy sayings, such as "You can observe a lot by watching." Today two of the best are Iván Rodríguez and Buster Posey. Rodríguez holds the record for catching the most games ever.

STAR PROFILE
BUSTER POSEY

28

Born: March 27, 1987 Leesburg, Georgia

Team: San Francisco Giants

Star Stats: 3x World Series champ, 1x National League MVP

HELMET

MASK

CHEST PROTECTOR

CATCHER'S MITT

SHIN GUARD

The catcher must wear extra gear as protection from balls and bats.

CLEATS

THE INFIELDERS

The pitcher can't strike out everyone. So what happens when the batter hits the ball? The infielders are the fielding team's first line of defense. If the batter hits a **grounder** or a **line drive**, the infielders take over.

Infielders turn a double play when they get two base runners out on the same play.

Tough Defense

A baseball club has four infielders: first baseman, second baseman, third baseman, and shortstop (between second and third base). Infielders try to get base runners out by tagging them or the base they are trying to reach. If an infielder makes a mistake, he or she is charged with an error and the batting team might score.

STAR PROFILE
OZZIE SMITH

Born: December 26, 1954
Mobile, Alabama

Teams: San Diego Padres,
St. Louis Cardinals

Star Stats: 2,511 games
played at shortstop,
13 straight shortstop
Gold Gloves, .978 fielding
percentage

WOW!
Infielder Cal Ripken, Jr.
has a legendary MLB
record—he played
for the Baltimore
Orioles in 2,632
consecutive games!

Most infielders have
smaller gloves than
outfielders. This helps
them get the ball out of
the glove more quickly.

Infield Idols

Infielders such as Ozzie Smith
and Mike Schmidt combined
solid defense with great
batting skills. Smith racked
up 2,460 hits and earned
13 Gold Gloves. Schmidt hit
548 homers while winning
10 Gold Gloves. Cal Ripken,
Jr. was another infielder
with impressive fielding
and batting **stats.**

The best infielders earn
the Gold Glove award.

THE OUTFIELDERS

When the batter hits the ball over the infield, the outfielders spring into action. They catch or chase down the ball to keep the other team from scoring.

WOW!

Baseball star Willie Mays won the Gold Glove 12 times!

Catching a fly ball is often an easy out for the outfielder's team. Other times outfielders need to do a lot of running to cover the gaps—those huge areas between the outfielders.

Back, Back, Back, Back!

The leftfielder, centerfielder, and rightfielder patrol an area that can measure more than 100 yards from the infield to the outfield fence. Outfielders must be fast to cover all that ground. They hope to catch **fly balls**. This is an easy way to make an out for their club.

Sometimes an outfielder makes a leaping catch at the fence, preventing a home run. This is why outfielders can earn Gold Gloves, too.

Outfielder Ty Cobb is one of baseball's all-time greats. His career hits record (4,191) stood for almost 60 years.

Old-Time Outfield

Many of baseball's best players have been outfielders. Ty Cobb set 90 MLB records during his career (1905–1928). And three of the greatest New York Yankees played the outfield: Babe Ruth, Mickey Mantle, and Joe DiMaggio. Together, they won 23 World Series and hit 1,611 home runs!

Outfield Aces

Other players continued the tradition of star outfielders. Rickey Henderson set MLB records for most stolen bases (1,406) and most runs scored (2,295). Tony Gwynn won five Gold Gloves and batted over .300 for 19 straight seasons! Today many of baseball's top stars, such as Andrew McCutchen and Mike Trout, play the outfield.

Andrew McCutchen is one of today's top young MLB outfielders.

THE MANAGER

Baseball involves a lot of strategy. The players need one person to lead them. That person is the manager. He leads from his club's dugout. A staff of coaches helps him.

Joe Torre was one of baseball's greatest managers. He led the New York Yankees from 1996 to 2007. During that time he won AL Manager of the Year twice.

Bench Boss

Baseball managers are former players. They have lots of knowledge of the game. A manager decides the order in which his players go to bat. He also chooses a pitcher to start the game. If the starter needs help, the manager sends in a reliever. Like the catcher, the manager uses hand signals to communicate with his players and other coaches. Sometimes, though, he can stop the game and talk to his players on the field.

Base coaches standing near first and third bases give instructions to the base runners.

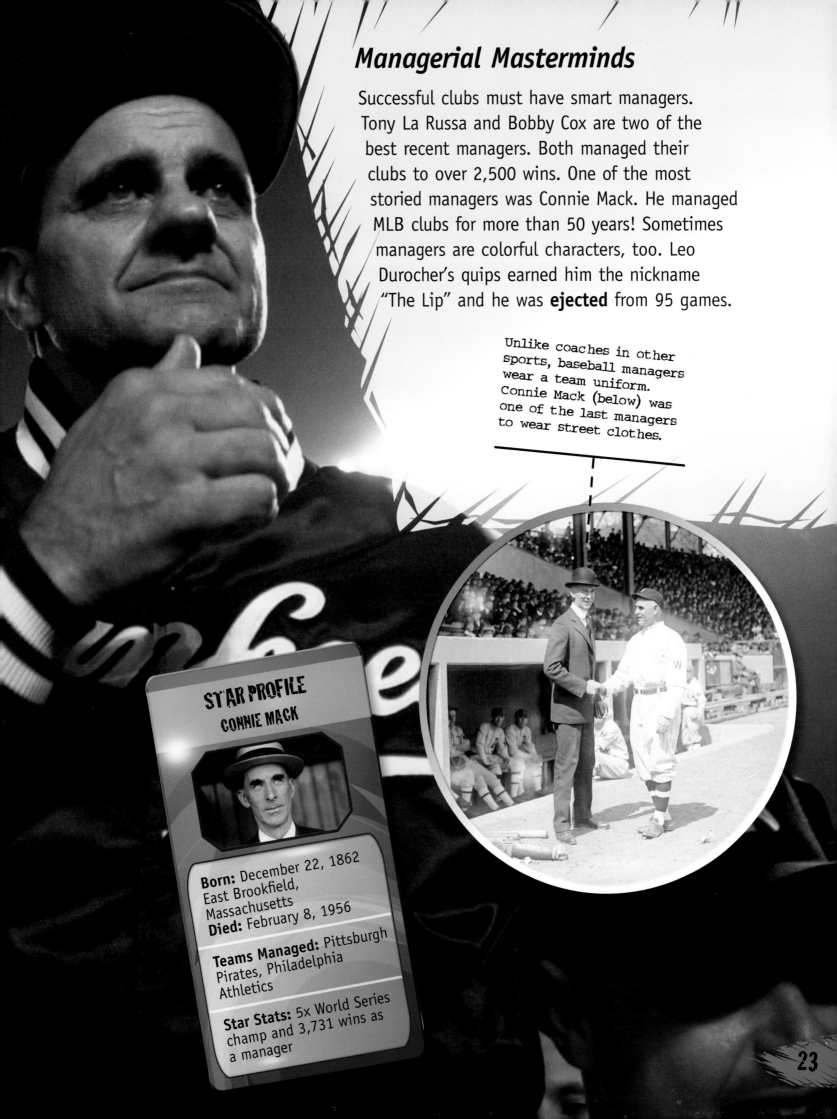

Managerial Masterminds

Successful clubs must have smart managers. Tony La Russa and Bobby Cox are two of the best recent managers. Both managed their clubs to over 2,500 wins. One of the most storied managers was Connie Mack. He managed MLB clubs for more than 50 years! Sometimes managers are colorful characters, too. Leo Durocher's quips earned him the nickname "The Lip" and he was **ejected** from 95 games.

Unlike coaches in other sports, baseball managers wear a team uniform. Connie Mack (below) was one of the last managers to wear street clothes.

STAR PROFILE
CONNIE MACK

Born: December 22, 1862 East Brookfield, Massachusetts
Died: February 8, 1956

Teams Managed: Pittsburgh Pirates, Philadelphia Athletics

Star Stats: 5x World Series champ and 3,731 wins as a manager

A SPORT FOR EVERYONE

In the last 150 years, baseball has spread around the globe. Today it is enjoyed by people with many different backgrounds. Baseball truly is a sport for everyone. But it wasn't always that way.

Baseball's popularity has spread around the globe. Here America's national pastime is enjoyed in the Dominican Republic.

Jackie Robinson

For many years, MLB teams would not hire black ballplayers. Then in 1947 Jackie Robinson played his first game with the Brooklyn Dodgers. He was the first African American to play in the MLB. Later that season another African American player, Larry Doby, joined the Cleveland Indians. Robinson and Doby faced the jeers of many white fans and even some teammates. It would take 12 years for every MLB club to integrate.

In 1947, Jackie Robinson became the first African American player in the Major Leagues. He played 10 seasons for the Brooklyn Dodgers.

STAR PROFILE
ROBERTO CLEMENTE

Born: August 18, 1934 San Juan, Puerto Rico
Died: December 31, 1972

Team: Pittsburgh Pirates

Star Stats: 15x All-Star, 2x World Series champ, 12x Gold Glove winner

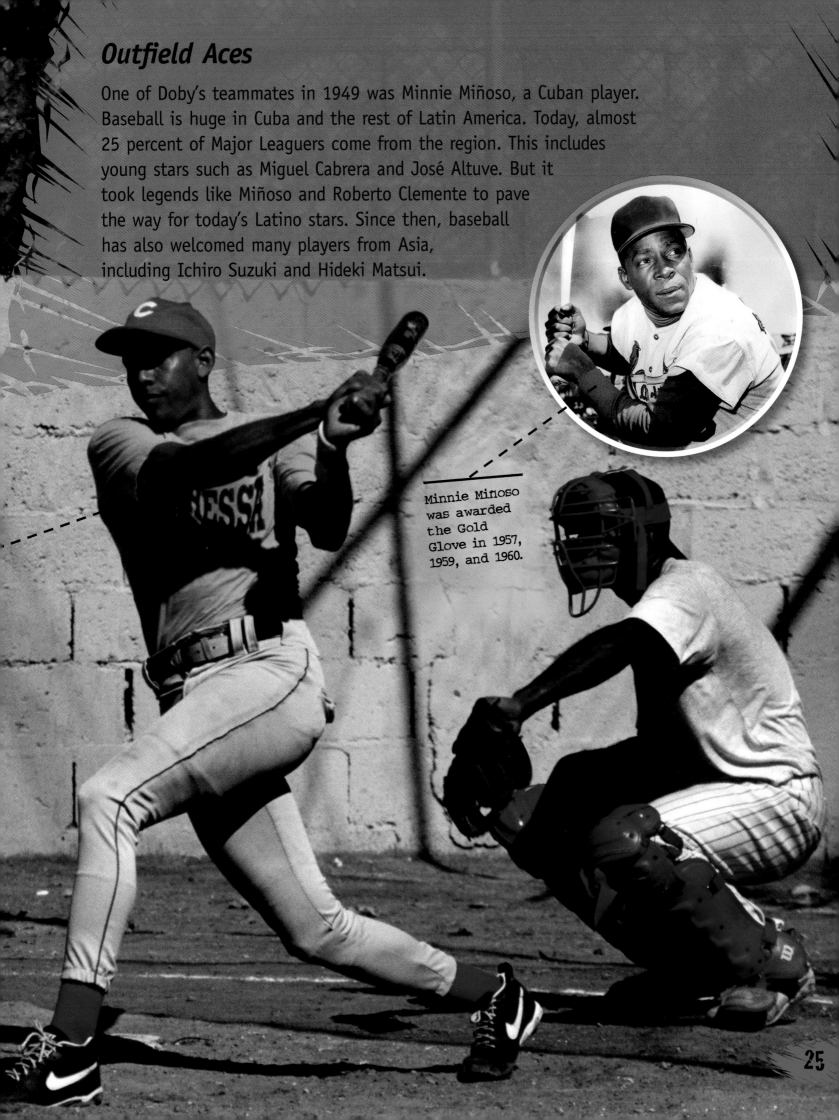

Outfield Aces

One of Doby's teammates in 1949 was Minnie Miñoso, a Cuban player. Baseball is huge in Cuba and the rest of Latin America. Today, almost 25 percent of Major Leaguers come from the region. This includes young stars such as Miguel Cabrera and José Altuve. But it took legends like Miñoso and Roberto Clemente to pave the way for today's Latino stars. Since then, baseball has also welcomed many players from Asia, including Ichiro Suzuki and Hideki Matsui.

Minnie Miñoso was awarded the Gold Glove in 1957, 1959, and 1960.

SCANDALS!

Baseball history isn't all about exciting games, great players, and smart managers. Baseball has a darker side too. Since the sport's early days players have occasionally gotten themselves into trouble.

Eddie Cicotte was one of eight players who were banned for life after the Black Sox scandal in the 1919 World Series.

The Black Sox Scandal

One of baseball's early scandals involved the 1919 Chicago White Sox. The team played the Cincinnati Reds in that year's World Series. Officials later discovered gamblers had paid Sox players to lose on purpose. Eight Sox players were banned from baseball for life. The 1919 team became known as the Black Sox. In 1989 another player was involved in a gambling scandal. Pete Rose, MLB's all-time hits leader, was banned from baseball for betting on games.

Pete Rose was nicknamed "Charlie Hustle" during his playing days.

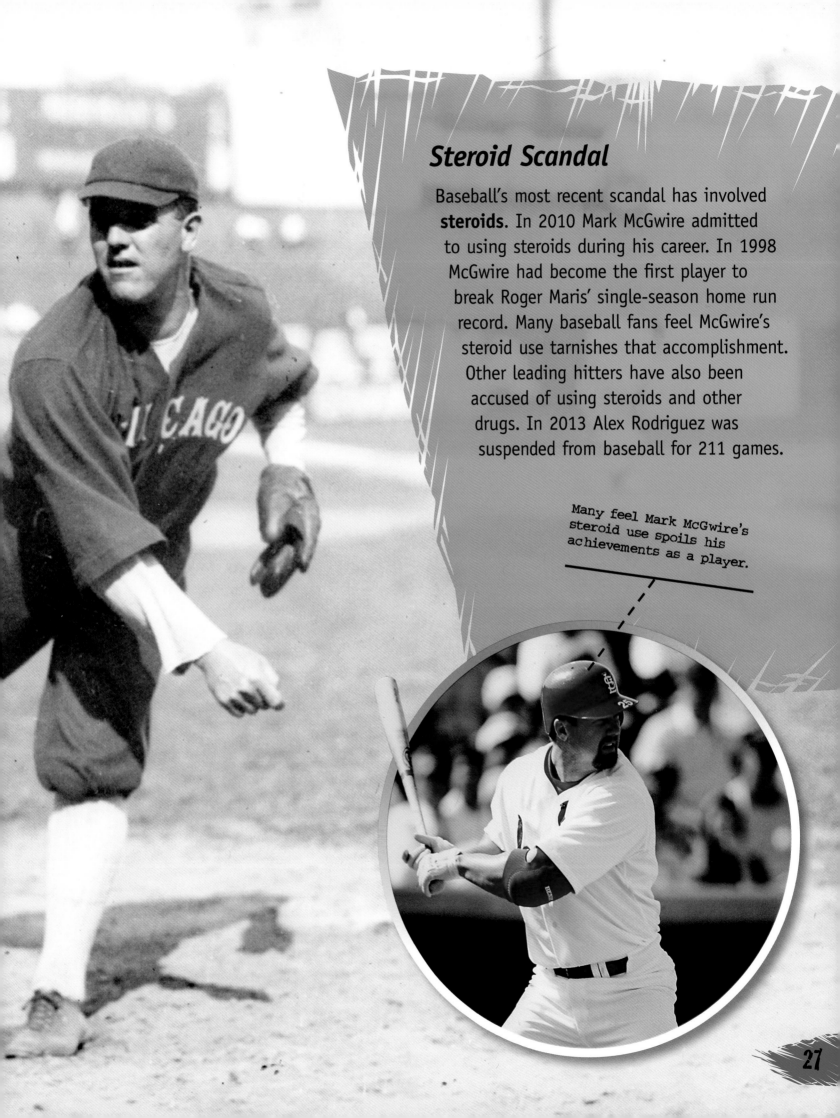

Steroid Scandal

Baseball's most recent scandal has involved **steroids**. In 2010 Mark McGwire admitted to using steroids during his career. In 1998 McGwire had become the first player to break Roger Maris' single-season home run record. Many baseball fans feel McGwire's steroid use tarnishes that accomplishment. Other leading hitters have also been accused of using steroids and other drugs. In 2013 Alex Rodriguez was suspended from baseball for 211 games.

Many feel Mark McGwire's steroid use spoils his achievements as a player.

THE WORLD SERIES

Every baseball player dreams of playing in the World Series. This championship contest is played every fall between the two top MLB teams. The "Fall Classic" is a best-of-seven event. The first team to win four games (more than half of seven) is the champion.

Watched by Millions

The first World Series was played in 1903. Teams across the USA (and from Toronto, Canada) have won the World Series but from 1921 to 1962, New York teams dominated play. The Yankees, Giants, and Dodgers combined to win 25 of 41 World Series! No matter who's playing, Americans love to watch on television. In 2014, an average of 13.8 million fans tuned in to each World Series game.

Willie Mays' amazing catch in Game 1 of the 1954 World Series is one of the most famous plays in baseball history.

Each year, the World Series champions are awarded the Commissioner's Trophy. This is Koji Uehara of the Boston Red Sox.

Who Plays?

In 1969 the MLB divided the American League (AL) and National League (NL) into East and West divisions. The winners from each moved on to the World Series. Today, both leagues have three divisions. Each division winner plus a **wild card** team in each league enters a playoff. The best teams from the AL and the NL playoffs go to the World Series.

Rightfielder Hunter Pence (#8 of the San Francisco Giants) runs to first base during Game 3 of the 2014 World Series.

STAR PROFILE
REGGIE "MR. OCTOBER" JACKSON

Born: May 18, 1946
Abington, Pennsylvania

Teams: Kansas City and Oakland Athletics, New York Yankees, Baltimore Orioles, California Angels

Star Stats: 27 games played, .457 batting average, 10 home runs

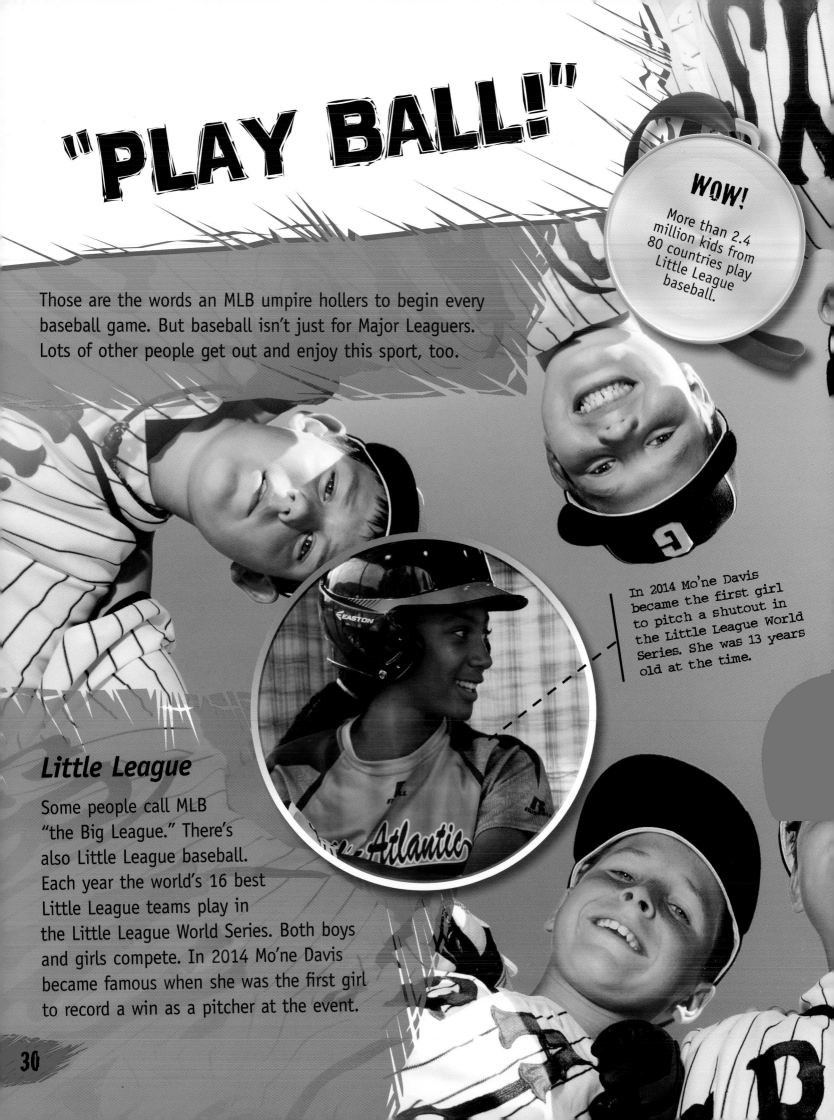

"PLAY BALL!"

Those are the words an MLB umpire hollers to begin every baseball game. But baseball isn't just for Major Leaguers. Lots of other people get out and enjoy this sport, too.

In 2014 Mo'ne Davis became the first girl to pitch a shutout in the Little League World Series. She was 13 years old at the time.

Little League

Some people call MLB "the Big League." There's also Little League baseball. Each year the world's 16 best Little League teams play in the Little League World Series. Both boys and girls compete. In 2014 Mo'ne Davis became famous when she was the first girl to record a win as a pitcher at the event.

30

Nearly every Big Leaguer learns the game of baseball as a kid, many of them while playing Little League baseball.

Women's softball is a very competitive and popular sport.

Kids and Grown-Ups

Before joining Little League some kids learn baseball by playing T-ball. And when they're older, adults across the nation enjoy softball, a baseball-like sport with slow pitches and a large ball. Today there are more than 200,000 softball teams in the USA, and more than four million players! Baseball is indeed a great game—just ask the millions of people who watch and play this fantastic sport.

FOOTBALL

Autumn in the United States means football! Every weekend fans cheer for their favorite teams. The only people more intense than the fans are the players! On the field, huge athletes collide, their protective gear crashing loudly in the cool air. From small fields to huge stadiums, football has come a long way. But some things have remained the same: football is still a fast, hard-hitting game full of strategy and teamwork.

Football is the most watched team sport in the USA. It is very popular at both the college and pro levels. Here, the Indianapolis Colts take on the Cincinnati Bengals.

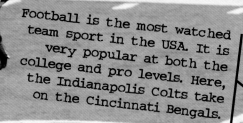

WOW!
More than 50 million people attended college football games in person in 2013.

FOOTBALL HISTORY

Just like baseball, football grew from other sports. American players added their own rules to other games. Over time, the sport became football as we know it today. But at first football was very violent. In the early 1900s, some even felt it should be outlawed.

Football grew out of college sports. This drawing shows the Yale and Columbia university teams playing in 1901. The leather helmets provided little protection against the game's violence.

Chaotic College Games

In the 1800s, teams from American colleges played sports that used rules from rugby and soccer. The first of these games was played in 1869 between Rutgers and Princeton. Every college had different rules. In 1873, a small group of colleges created one set of rules to follow. These rules allowed 20 players per team to be on the field. Games could be brutal.

In football's early days players wore only shirts and perhaps thinly padded pants. This is the 1891 Rutgers team.

WOW!
In 1905 19 men were killed and more than 150 were injured playing football.

Game Changers

Walter Camp is considered "the father of American football." Camp played for Yale University. In 1880 he introduced the **hike**, or the "snap," to football. He also suggested that each team have 11 players on the field and proposed a system of downs. In 1905, US President Teddy Roosevelt called a summit of football advisors to help make football less dangerous. His own son had been badly injured playing for Harvard. The field was reduced to its current size and the forward pass was made legal.

Walter Camp is credited for suggesting many rule changes that today's football fans take for granted.

KICKOFF TIME

Some football games are played in huge stadiums before 100,000 fans. Others are played in small parks with just a few spectators. But from youth levels all the way to the National Football League (NFL), teams play on a field with the same measurements and follow the same general rules.

The Football Field

Football games take place on a field. The playing area is 100 yards long and there are two 10-yard-long end zones. Games begin with a **kickoff** and are split into four 15-minute quarters.

The playing area is marked with a white line every yard and a number every ten yards.

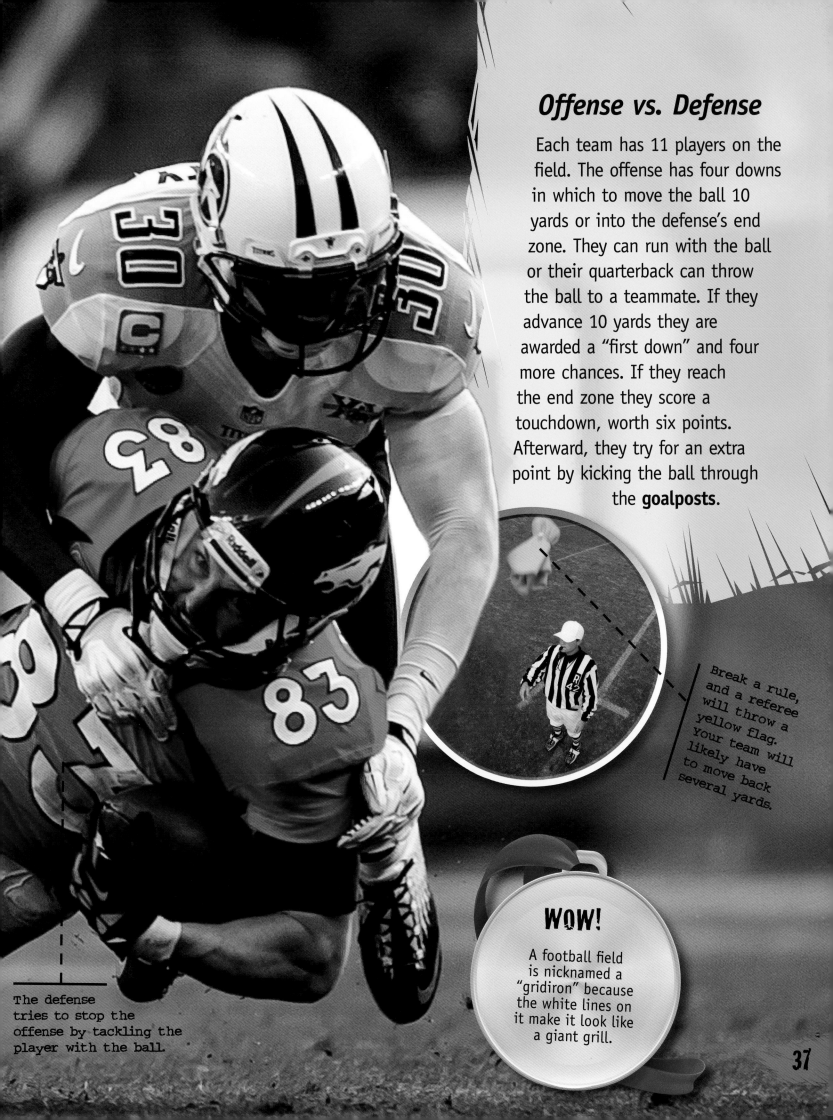

Offense vs. Defense

Each team has 11 players on the field. The offense has four downs in which to move the ball 10 yards or into the defense's end zone. They can run with the ball or their quarterback can throw the ball to a teammate. If they advance 10 yards they are awarded a "first down" and four more chances. If they reach the end zone they score a touchdown, worth six points. Afterward, they try for an extra point by kicking the ball through the **goalposts**.

Break a rule, and a referee will throw a yellow flag. Your team will likely have to move back several yards.

The defense tries to stop the offense by tackling the player with the ball.

WOW!

A football field is nicknamed a "gridiron" because the white lines on it make it look like a giant grill.

37

FOOTBALL EQUIPMENT

Make no mistake: football is a rough sport. Defensive players try to **tackle** the player with the ball. Offensive players can prevent this by blocking the defensive players. Several pieces of gear are used by football players of all levels.

HIP PAD

SHOE WITH STUDS

THIGH PAD

KNEE PAD

WOW!

Workers at the Wilson Football factory in Ohio make 4,000 footballs a day and more than 700,000 a year!

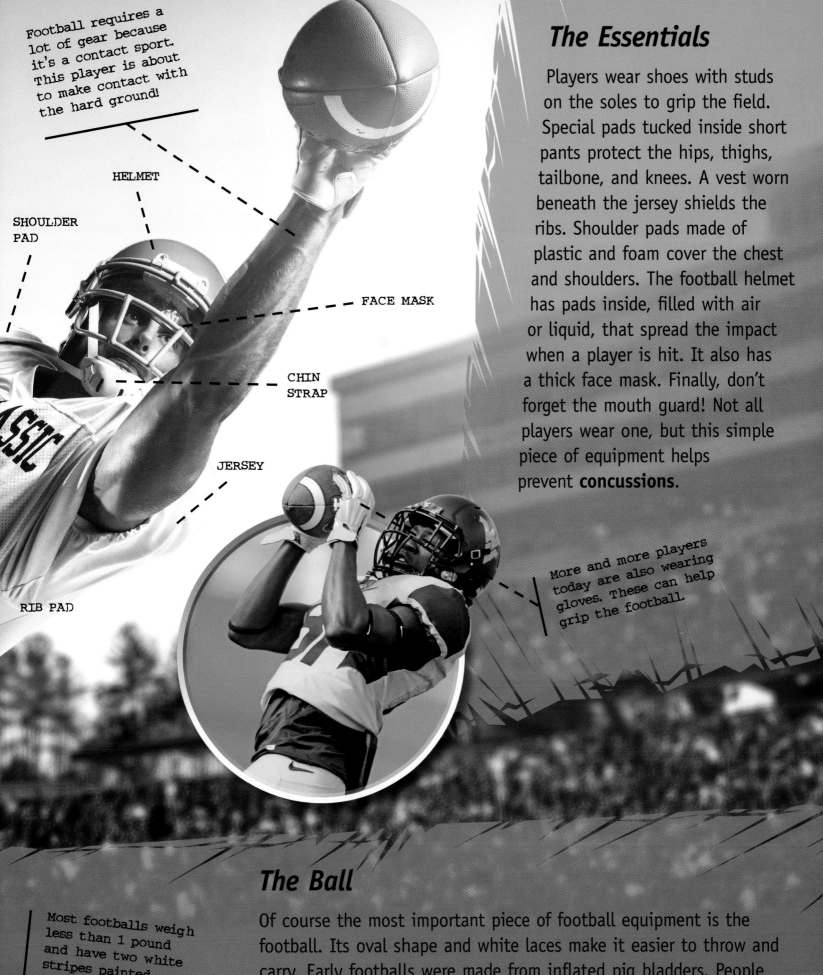

Football requires a lot of gear because it's a contact sport. This player is about to make contact with the hard ground!

HELMET

SHOULDER PAD

FACE MASK

CHIN STRAP

JERSEY

RIB PAD

The Essentials

Players wear shoes with studs on the soles to grip the field. Special pads tucked inside short pants protect the hips, thighs, tailbone, and knees. A vest worn beneath the jersey shields the ribs. Shoulder pads made of plastic and foam cover the chest and shoulders. The football helmet has pads inside, filled with air or liquid, that spread the impact when a player is hit. It also has a thick face mask. Finally, don't forget the mouth guard! Not all players wear one, but this simple piece of equipment helps prevent **concussions**.

More and more players today are also wearing gloves. These can help grip the football

The Ball

Most footballs weigh less than 1 pound and have two white stripes painted around them. Stripes improve the ball's visibility—especially in nighttime games.

Of course the most important piece of football equipment is the football. Its oval shape and white laces make it easier to throw and carry. Early footballs were made from inflated pig bladders. People called them "pigskins"—a nickname still used today. Today, footballs are made of cowhide or rubber. A pebbly texture is stamped onto them to make them easy to grip.

THE QUARTERBACK

Football features a lot of positions. Eleven players are on the field for each team. Each of those players must do his job perfectly for the team to succeed. Let's take a look at these positions, beginning with the quarterback.

Together with the coach, the quarterback chooses the play.

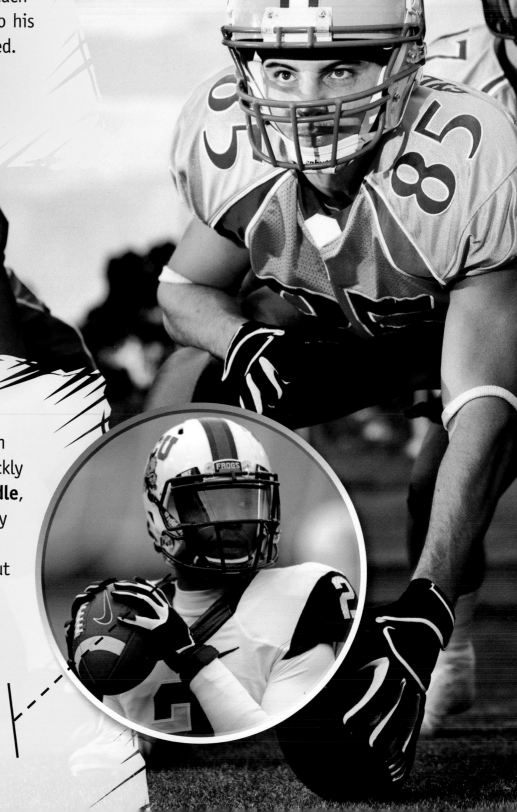

Field General

The quarterback leads the offense on the field. On each play he must quickly recognize the situation. In the **huddle**, he tells his teammates what the play will be. If the defense changes its strategy, the quarterback might shout an audible—a coded instruction to change the play. No wonder the quarterback is sometimes called the "field general!"

Some players, including quarterbacks, wear a clear visor on their helmet. This protects the eyes and improves visibility.

QB Greats

Many of the most popular NFL players have been quarterbacks. One of the early greats was George Blanda, who played an incredible 26 pro seasons (1949–1975). He still holds more than 10 records. Johnny Unitas also enjoyed a long career (1955–1973). He was named the NFL most valuable player (MVP) four times. Today, two of the NFL's most successful quarterbacks—and biggest stars—are Tom Brady and Peyton Manning. But soon a new crop of legends will take over.

Until the 1940s, footballers played both offense and defense. Sammy Baugh was quarterback, punter, and defensive back for the Washington Redskins from 1937 to 1952.

STAR PROFILE
JOE MONTANA

Born: June 11, 1956 New Eagle, Pennsylvania

Teams: San Francisco 49ers, Kansas City Chiefs

Star Stats: 4x Super Bowl champion, 3x MVP

WOW!

Brett Favre holds the record for most career passing yards: 71,838. That equals nearly 41 miles!

THE RUNNING BACKS

Rushing plays are among the most common in football. On these plays, the quarterback hands the ball to a running back. Some running backs try to use their speed to get *around* the defense. Others try to use their size to go *through* the defense.

Many football fans consider Emmitt Smith to be the best running back of all time.

Fullbacks and Halfbacks

Before a play, running backs line up in the backfield behind the quarterback. There are two running back positions: fullback and halfback (sometimes called tailbacks). Fullbacks are usually bigger. They block for the halfback more than they carry the ball. Halfbacks take **handoffs**, but sometimes they catch short passes, too. For any running back, 100 rushing yards in one game is a top-notch performance.

Jim Thorpe played eight pro seasons in the 1920s. He also played pro baseball and won two Olympic gold medals in 1912! As a college running back he once scored 198 points in a single season.

Stars of the Backfield

Because they carry the ball so much, running backs have been some of football's biggest stars. Jim Brown played nine seasons (1957–1965) and was the NFL rushing champion for eight of them. Walter Payton was another great. His running style earned the nickname "Sweetness." Today, young stars like Marshawn Lynch and LeSean McCoy excite pro football fans with their rushing skills.

LeSean McCoy, one of the NFL's best running backs, avoids a tackler.

WOW!

In 2014 Samaje Perine of the University of Oklahoma set a college record by rushing for 427 yards in a single game!

WIDE RECEIVERS

Instead of taking handoffs, wide receivers catch passes. Passes can be as short as a few yards or 50 yards or more. Wide receivers make some of the most exciting plays in football.

STAR PROFILE
JERRY RICE

Born: October 13, 1962 Starkville, Mississippi

Teams: San Francisco 49ers, Oakland Raiders, Seattle Seahawks

Star Stats: 22,895 career receiving yards, 1,549 career receptions (both NFL records)

WOW!

The NFL record for most touchdown catches in one game is five. Three players share the record.

Brandon Pettigrew of the NFL's Detroit Lions makes a diving catch against the New England Patriots.

Going Deep

Passing plays have different routes. This is the pattern the wide receiver runs. The quarterback throws the ball so the receiver can catch it at the end of his route. This requires perfect timing. Some plays call for inside routes—the receiver runs to the middle of the field for a catch. Other plays have outside routes, where the receiver "goes deep" down a **sideline**. The receiver makes a "reception" if he catches the ball.

One-handed catches are spectacular, but players learn to catch a football with two hands..

Kings of the Catch

Wide receivers are great runners. They also are some of football's most dynamic players. Randy Moss played 14 seasons, and achieved the NFL's second most regular season touchdown catches: 256. One of today's great receivers is Calvin Johnson, nicknamed "Megatron." In 2012 he caught an amazing 122 passes. But Jerry Rice is considered the greatest wide receiver ever. He once owned more than 100 NFL records!

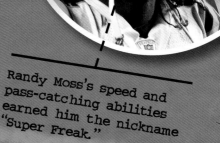

Randy Moss's speed and pass-catching abilities earned him the nickname "Super Freak."

45

THE LINEMEN

Unlike other offensive linemen, the tight end is allowed to catch passes.

The largest of all football players are the linemen. College and NFL linemen are usually taller than 6 feet. Many weigh more than 300 pounds. What do these players do that requires them to be so enormous?

STAR PROFILE
BRUCE SMITH

Born: June 18, 1963 Norfolk, Virginia

Teams: Buffalo Bills, Washington Redskins

Star Stats: 200 career sacks (NFL record), 11x Pro Bowl selection

WOW!

Aaron Gibson played in the NFL from 1999 to 2005. He stood 6 feet, 9 inches and weighed more than 400 pounds.

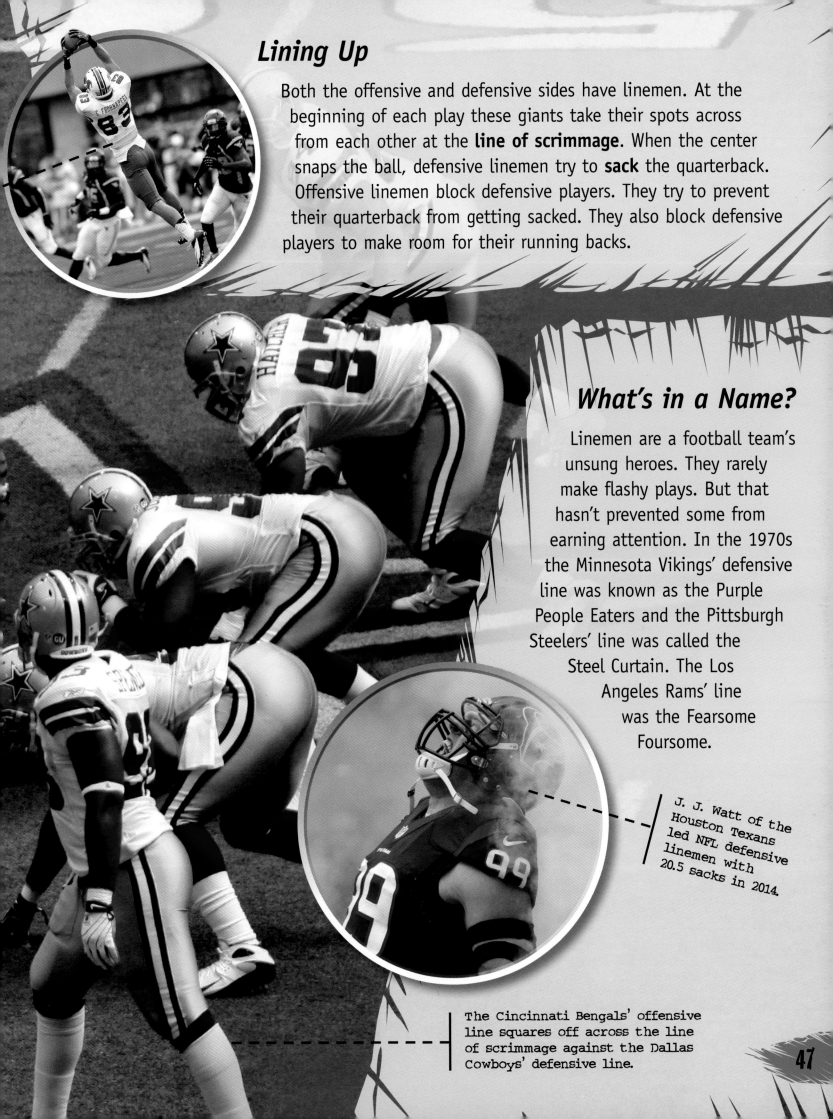

Lining Up

Both the offensive and defensive sides have linemen. At the beginning of each play these giants take their spots across from each other at the **line of scrimmage**. When the center snaps the ball, defensive linemen try to **sack** the quarterback. Offensive linemen block defensive players. They try to prevent their quarterback from getting sacked. They also block defensive players to make room for their running backs.

What's in a Name?

Linemen are a football team's unsung heroes. They rarely make flashy plays. But that hasn't prevented some from earning attention. In the 1970s the Minnesota Vikings' defensive line was known as the Purple People Eaters and the Pittsburgh Steelers' line was called the Steel Curtain. The Los Angeles Rams' line was the Fearsome Foursome.

J. J. Watt of the Houston Texans led NFL defensive linemen with 20.5 sacks in 2014

The Cincinnati Bengals' offensive line squares off across the line of scrimmage against the Dallas Cowboys' defensive line.

LINEBACKERS & DEFENSIVE BACKS

Sometimes running backs break past the line of scrimmage or wide receivers streak down the field. This is when linebackers and defensive backs get in on the action.

WOW!
Linebacker Ray Lewis played 17 seasons for the Baltimore Ravens and made 1,336 tackles.

One linebacker directs the defense while on the field. Clay Matthews (#52) of the Green Bay Packers is a star NFL linebacker.

Last Lines of Defense

Linebackers start the play about 5 yards behind the line of scrimmage. One linebacker directs the defense, much like the quarterback on offense. Defensive backs cover wide receivers running downfield. These "d-backs" can catch the ball, too. If they do, they get an interception and their team's offense gets the ball back.

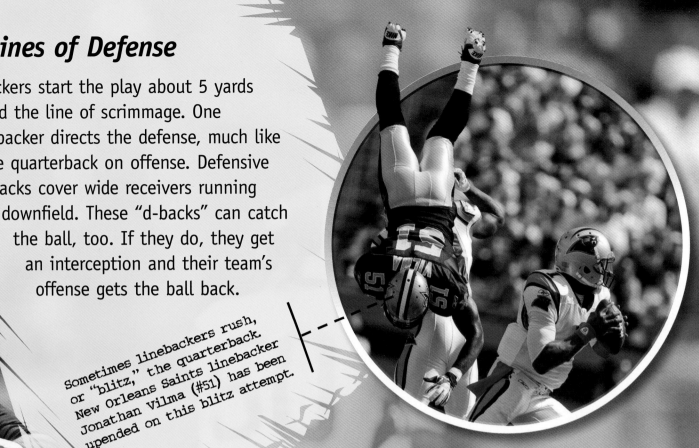

Sometimes linebackers rush, or "blitz," the quarterback. New Orleans Saints linebacker Jonathan Vilma (#51) has been upended on this blitz attempt.

Ray Lewis was one of the most feared linebackers in the NFL. He retired in 2013.

STAR PROFILE
DICK BUTKUS

Born: December 9, 1942 Chicago, Illinois

Team: Chicago Bears

Star Stats: 1,020 career tackles

Bruising LBs

Paul Krause set the NFL record for interceptions—he made 81 during his career with the Washington Redskins (1964–1967) and Minnesota Vikings (1968–1979). Lawrence Taylor of the New York Giants (1981–1993) was known for fearsome tackles but he could also make sacks on the **blitz** or drop back for an interception. The Baltimore Ravens' Ray Lewis was selected for 13 Pro Bowls—a linebacker record. Today's top young linebacker might be Luke Kuechly. In 2012 he made 103 tackles and was named NFL Defensive Rookie of the Year.

PLACEKICKERS & PUNTERS

Talk about pressure! If a game is tied in the game's final seconds and his team is close to the goal line, the placekicker is called in. If he kicks a field goal through the goalposts, his team will win the game. But if he misses . . .

Golden Feet

After his team scores a touchdown, a placekicker attempts an extra point. Usually when his team reaches fourth down near the opponent's end zone, he tries for a field goal, worth three points. The punter is another **special teams** player. When his team is too far away to try for a field goal on fourth down, it's his job to **drop-kick** the ball to the opponent.

Punter Ray Guy once hit a video screen hanging from the ceiling of the Superdome with a punt.

WOW!
The longest field goal in NFL history was 64 yards, kicked by Matt Prater of the Denver Broncos on December 8, 2013.

Top Scorers

Kickers score only one or three points at a time. But over many years, those points can add up. The top 31 scorers in NFL history are placekickers! The two greatest of all time are Morten Andersen (2,544 points) and Gary Anderson (2,434 points). Both began their NFL careers in 1982, and both were experienced soccer players before playing American football.

Morten Andersen is the NFL's all-time leading scorer. He played for six teams, including the Minnesota Vikings.

STAR PROFILE
MORTEN ANDERSEN

Born: August 16, 1960 Copenhagen, Denmark

Teams: New Orleans Saints, Atlanta Falcons, New York Giants, Kansas City Chiefs, Minnesota Vikings

Star Stats: 2,544 career points, 382 games played (both NFL records)

The ball is kicked to the opposing team to begin a game or after one team has scored. For these "kickoffs," the kicker sets the ball on a rubber tee.

THE COACH

We've seen that a football team has a lot of players. We also learned that football is a sport of strategy and teamwork. So who directs these players and decides on a strategy? That job belongs to the head coach.

Brains behind the Brawn

A football coach can't guide a team alone. He has a large group of assistants. Some coaches help players get better at their position. Others, called coordinators, guide the offense, the defense, and special teams. Before the season the coaches create a **playbook**. This contains the plays the team will use during the season. The plays drawn on its pages use Xs and Os to represent the players.

Coaches use diagrams to teach plays to their team. Os represent the offense; Xs are the defense.

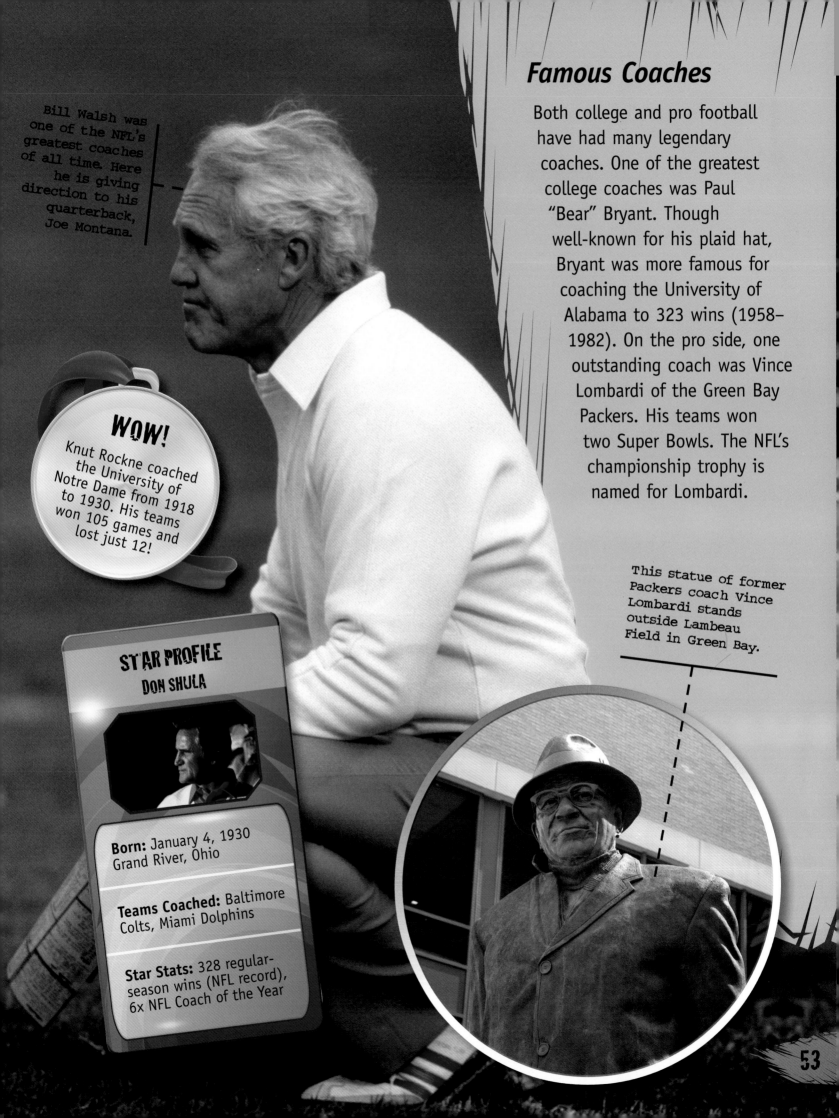

Bill Walsh was one of the NFL's greatest coaches of all time. Here he is giving direction to his quarterback, Joe Montana.

Famous Coaches

Both college and pro football have had many legendary coaches. One of the greatest college coaches was Paul "Bear" Bryant. Though well-known for his plaid hat, Bryant was more famous for coaching the University of Alabama to 323 wins (1958–1982). On the pro side, one outstanding coach was Vince Lombardi of the Green Bay Packers. His teams won two Super Bowls. The NFL's championship trophy is named for Lombardi.

WOW!

Knut Rockne coached the University of Notre Dame from 1918 to 1930. His teams won 105 games and lost just 12!

This statue of former Packers coach Vince Lombardi stands outside Lambeau Field in Green Bay.

STAR PROFILE
DON SHULA

Born: January 4, 1930 Grand River, Ohio

Teams Coached: Baltimore Colts, Miami Dolphins

Star Stats: 328 regular-season wins (NFL record), 6x NFL Coach of the Year

COLLEGE FOOTBALL

Few sports in the USA are as popular as college football. Hundreds of American colleges and universities have football teams. Every Saturday afternoon throughout the fall, these teams square off at stadiums across the country.

Oregon quarterback Marcus Mariota (#8) runs the ball against UCLA. The Oregon Ducks are one of college football's top teams.

WOW!

Of the 20 largest stadiums in the USA, 16 are the homes of college football teams.

Bowl-Bound

American football had its start at the college level. Today, the top college teams compete in the Football Bowl Subdivision (FBS). Most NFL players first play for FBS teams. FBS teams with winning records are chosen to play in bowl games at the end of the season. The winning teams from two of those bowl games go on to play for the national championship.

Utah and Georgia Tech play in the 2011 Sun Bowl. A team with a good record generally earns a place in a bowl game.

STAR PROFILE
HAROLD "RED" GRANGE

Born: June 13, 1903 Forksville, Pennsylvania
Died: January 28, 1991

Team: University of Illinois

Star Stats: 3,362 rushing yards, 31 touchdowns, 3x All-American

Heisman Heroes and Zeroes

Each year the most outstanding player in college football is awarded the Heisman Trophy. This award started in 1935. Most often, a quarterback or running back wins it. Some go on to enjoy careers in the NFL, but not all of them! Several Heisman winners, especially quarterbacks, have failed at the NFL level. Some call this the "Heisman Curse," even though many other winners have enjoyed long NFL careers.

Auburn quarterback Cam Newton won the 2010 Heisman Trophy. The Heisman is made of bronze and weighs 25 pounds.

THE SUPER BOWL

The Super Bowl is the biggest spectacle in American sports. Each February, more than 100 million Americans watch this game on television. No wonder! In the Super Bowl, two NFL teams compete for the right to be called the best team in football.

Super History

The first Super Bowl was played in 1967. It was originally a game between the champions of the American Football League and the National Football League. By 1970, the leagues had combined into one, and the Super Bowl continued. Over the years, a number of **dynasties** have won multiple Super Bowls. But the NFL team with the most Super Bowl titles is the Pittsburgh Steelers with six.

Some people look forward to the Super Bowl halftime show as much as the game itself. Here, singer Katy Perry performs at the Super Bowl in Glendale, Arizona, on February 1, 2015.

More than 350,000 fans braved the cold to congratulate the Pittsburgh Steelers at their 2009 Super Bowl victory parade.

STAR PROFILE
TOM BRADY

Born: August 3, 1977 San Mateo, California

Team: New England Patriots

Star Stats: 4x Super Bowl champ, 3x Super Bowl MVP

Who Plays?

The NFL has two conferences: the National Football Conference (NFC) and the American Football Conference (AFC). Each conference has 16 teams. The top six teams in each conference enter the playoffs. When a team loses, their season ends. The last two unbeaten playoff teams—one NFC team and one AFC team—meet in the Super Bowl. The game is played at a **neutral site**.

The Lombardi Trophy is awarded to the winning Super Bowl team.

WOW!
If everyone who watched the 2015 Super Bowl stood fingertip to fingertip with their arms outstretched, they would circle the Earth four-and-a-half times.

READY FOR SOME FOOTBALL?

College and pro football may be hugely popular in the USA, but others are enjoying time on the field, too. From grade school to high school and beyond, football fans are also playing the game.

WOW!

More than 52,000 fans gathered at AT&T Stadium in Arlington, Texas, in 2014 to watch a championship high school football game.

Turn Off the TV!

Football's a great sport for television. But many people enjoy playing, not just watching. Some families have a tradition of "touch" football games on Thanksgiving. The ball carrier is down when a defender touches them with two hands. And a lot of players start their careers with flag football. Instead of tackling, defensive players try to grab a flag from the ball carrier's belt.

In flag football, when a player has a strip of cloth, or "flag," torn from their belt, he or she is "down."

These youngsters are among the 250,000 kids who play Pop Warner League youth football in the USA.

STAR PROFILE
GLENN "POP" WARNER

Born: April 5, 1871 Chicago, Illinois
Died: September 7, 1954

Teams Coached: Georgia, Iowa State, Cornell, Carlisle, Pittsburgh, Stanford, Temple

Star Stats: 319 wins, 106 losses, 32 ties

Pop Warner

More than a quarter of a million youngsters also join Pop Warner football, named for the great college football coach. Thousands of teens play for their high school teams. High school football is especially big in states like Texas and Florida. No doubt about it, football is a great American sport. And its popularity only seems to grow!

Just like pro players, Pop Warner teams play the game no matter how muddy the field might be!

BASKETBALL

Basketball has humble beginnings in a sweaty old gymnasium. Today it is enjoyed throughout the USA and elsewhere. From public parks to gleaming arenas, boys, girls, women, and men play the sport. Every March men's and women's college basketball tournaments excite fans like no others. And throughout the year the professional National Basketball Association (NBA) and Women's National Basketball Association (WNBA) entertain fans across the country.

Villanova forward Laura Sweeney (#33) dribbles against West Virginia guard Asya Bussie (#20). There are 348 schools that sponsor women's basketball teams at the college game's top level.

61

THE HISTORY OF BASKETBALL

Basketball is a popular summertime playground sport. Most basketball leagues, however, hold their seasons during the winter months. This goes back all the way to the invention of basketball.

WOW!

The first basketball game was played on January 20, 1892. The final score? 1-0!

A Cold Start

Dr. James Naismith was a **physical education** professor in Springfield, Massachusetts. Naismith came up with an indoor game to keep his students active during the long, cold winters. In December 1891 he nailed two peach baskets to the balcony that circled the school's gymnasium. Teams tried to toss a soccer ball into the opposing team's peach basket. Naismith called his new game "basket ball."

Naismith was photographed with his first basketball team in 1891.

STAR PROFILE
JAMES NAISMITH

Born: November 6, 1861 Ontario, Canada
Died: November 28, 1939

Team Coached: University of Kansas

Star Stat: Incredibly, Naismith had a losing record (55 wins, 60 losses) as head basketball coach at the University of Kansas!

Changing the Game

At first, each team had nine players. A few years later, Naismith reduced the teams to five players each. He also added **backboards** behind the baskets. He found fans in the balcony could reach down and knock away the opposing team's shots!

The US Basketball Hall of Fame is located in Springfield, Massachusetts, in honor of James Naismith.

TIPOFF

Basketball is played on a court. Most basketball courts are inside gymnasiums and arenas and have wood floors. But basketball courts can also be found outdoors in parks and schoolyards, where they have asphalt, concrete, or even dirt surfaces.

The basket's rim is 10 feet above the floor. Still, many players are able to dunk the ball—jump up and stuff it through the rim.

Hardwood and Hoops

College and pro courts are 94 feet long and 50 feet wide. Younger teams play on smaller courts. The court's floor is made of hard polished wood. At each end there is a circular rim with a net called a basket. The rim is 10 feet above the court. Because the rim is so high, tall athletes often excel at basketball.

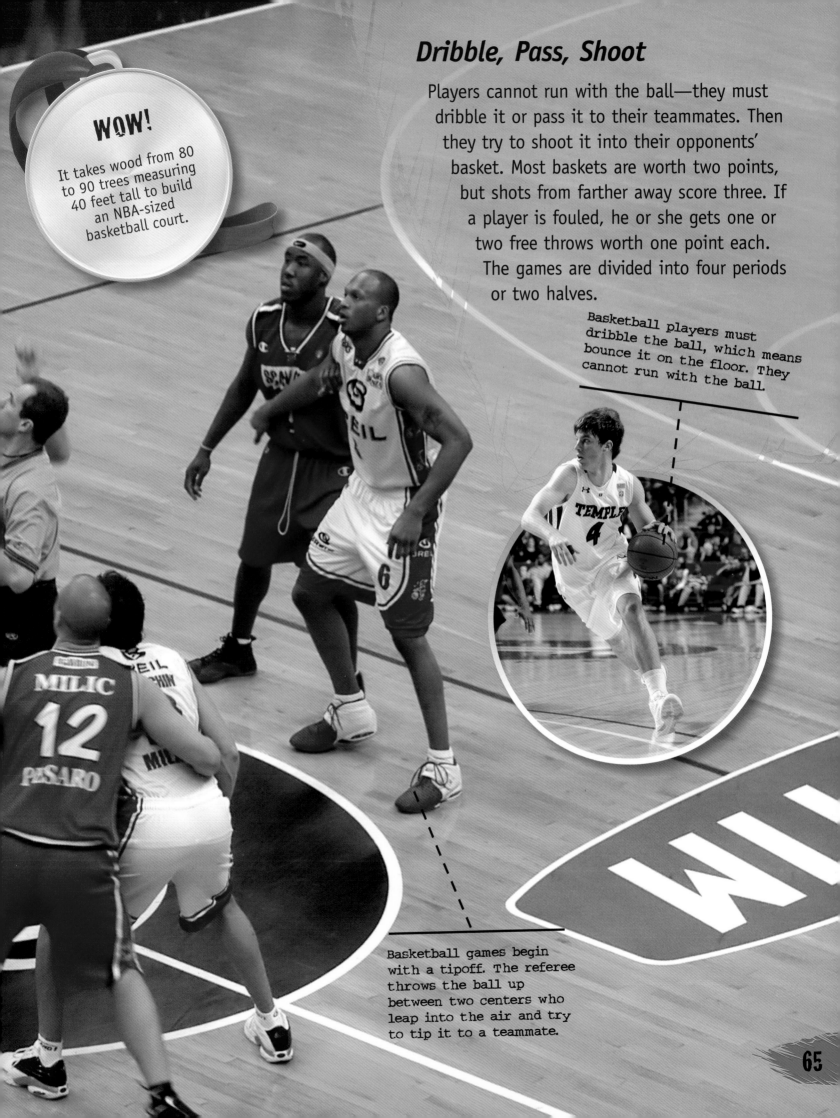

Dribble, Pass, Shoot

Players cannot run with the ball—they must dribble it or pass it to their teammates. Then they try to shoot it into their opponents' basket. Most baskets are worth two points, but shots from farther away score three. If a player is fouled, he or she gets one or two free throws worth one point each. The games are divided into four periods or two halves.

Basketball players must dribble the ball, which means bounce it on the floor. They cannot run with the ball.

Basketball games begin with a tipoff. The referee throws the ball up between two centers who leap into the air and try to tip it to a teammate.

BASKETBALL EQUIPMENT

Basketball's popularity has spread around the world. One reason is the equipment—you don't need a lot of it to enjoy the sport. A lot of parks have outdoor courts. And many gyms offer **pickup** games. All you need are a pair of sneakers and a friend with a ball.

Perfectly Round

"Roundball" is a slang term for the sport of basketball. That's because a basketball is shaped like a perfect sphere. It's about 30 inches around and usually orange in color with black lines, or ribs. Balls with a leather covering are best for indoor games. For playing outdoors, it's better to use one made of a tough material such as rubber. Dribbling a leather ball on asphalt can quickly ruin it.

The black lines on a basketball are called its ribs. This is a tough, outdoor ball.

BASKETBALL

---- JERSEY

SHORTS

Super Sneakers

The other piece of gear needed for basketball is a comfortable pair of sneakers. Basketball sneakers have evolved a lot from the sport's early days. They used to be made of canvas with rubber soles. Today's players wear sneakers made of leather. Most players prefer sneakers that cover the ankles. These offer better support when jumping and landing.

Today's basketball sneakers are made of leather and have sturdy rubber soles. They are also usually "high tops" to support the athlete's ankles.

Famous for their red, white, and blue ball, the Harlem Globetrotters are a favorite worldwide. They usually take on the Washington Generals, seen here.

67

THE CENTER

A basketball team has five players on the court. They work together on offense to score baskets. When their opponents have the ball, they play defense and try to prevent them from making baskets. One of the five players is the center, sometimes called the "big man" in the NBA.

WOW!

Centers Manute Bol and Gheorghe Muresan were the NBA's tallest players to date. Both stood 7 feet, 7 inches tall.

Many fans believe Marc Gasol (#33) of the Memphis Grizzlies is the NBA's best center.

SPALDING

PERFORMX

Middle of the Action

The center is often a team's tallest player. On defense, the center usually hangs around his or her team's basket. When the other team misses a shot, the center tries to get the **rebound**. The center may also block shots. On offense, the center plays near the other team's basket. He or she battles for offensive rebounds and takes short shots. Occasionally the center makes a **slam dunk**, too.

Kevin McHale played both center and forward for the Boston Celtics.

Wilt Chamberlain's most remarkable record is scoring 100 points in a single game.

STAR PROFILE
KAREEM ABDUL-JABBAR

Born: April 16, 1947
New York City, New York

Teams: Milwaukee Bucks, Los Angeles Lakers

Star Stats: 38,387 points, 6x MVP (both NBA records)

NBA Big Men

George Mikan was the NBA's first big man. He played for the Minneapolis Lakers in the 1950s. Many centers followed in his footsteps. Wilt Chamberlain played from 1959 to 1973 and still holds the NBA record for most rebounds (23,924). But his greatest record is scoring 100 points in one game! Shaquille O'Neal, another great center, scored at least 20 points and made 10 rebounds per game.

69

THE POWER FORWARD

There are two forward positions in basketball: power forward and small forward. Some of their jobs, like rebounding and blocking shots, overlap with the center's jobs. And like everyone on the team, they must pitch in on both offense and defense.

Forward Rebekkah Brunson dribbles the ball toward the basket in a European league game. Many WNBA players compete in European leagues during the WNBA's off season.

WOW!

Kevin Garnett has topped 25,000 points, 10,000 rebounds, 5,000 **assists**, 1,500 steals, and 1,500 blocked shots in his career—the only NBA player so far to do so.

Power forward Tim Duncan grabs an offensive rebound against the Nets, formerly of New Jersey.

Power Up

On offense, a power forward plays near the basket, watching his or her teammates. If a teammate shoots, the power forward knows to be ready for an offensive rebound. On defense, the power forward might play under his or her basket and help their team scoop up defensive rebounds. If their team plays a man-to-man defense, they cover one of the other team's forwards instead.

Power Players

Karl Malone helped define the power forward position. Malone was known as "the Mailman," because it was said he always delivered. He holds the record for second most career points (36,928). Charles Barkley was another impressive power forward. "Sir Charles" was also effective at scoring and rebounding. Today, two of the best power forwards play for Texas teams: Dirk Nowitzki of the Dallas Mavericks and Tim Duncan of the San Antonio Spurs.

STAR PROFILE
TIM DUNCAN

Born: April 25, 1976 Christiansted, US Virgin Islands

Team: San Antonio Spurs

Star Stats: 5x NBA champ, one of two players to win NBA championship in three decades (1990s, 2000s, 2010s)

Power forward Dirk Nowitzki stands 7 feet tall. He joined the Dallas Mavericks in 1998, and has led his team to 14 NBA playoffs.

THE SMALL FORWARD

Basketball's other forward position is small forward. Like their name suggests, small forwards usually aren't as big as power forwards. That's because their role is a bit different. It requires a little more speed than the power forward position.

A Bit of Everything

Often, the small forward can be seen dribbling the ball toward the opponent's basket. The small forward is also a good passer, giving the ball to teammates when he or she doesn't have a good scoring chance. When they do shoot, they tend to take most of their shots from farther out than the center. Small forwards also get rebounds if they can. In other words, they do a bit of everything.

WOW!
Small forward Alex English led the NBA in scoring during the 1980s with 19,682 points—despite never winning a league championship.

LeBron James is the premier small forward in basketball today. Here he is dribbling the ball up the court.

Small forward Kevin Durant is one of the brightest stars in the NBA today.

Famous Forwards

Two of basketball's greatest players were considered small forwards. Julius "Dr. J" Erving played 17 pro seasons and was famous for his high-flying slam dunks. Larry Bird was less flashy, but helped the Boston Celtics win three championships in the 1980s. He later coached the Indiana Pacers. Today, the game's biggest star often plays small forward. LeBron James has been on two championship teams and is a four-time NBA MVP. And he went straight from high school to the pros!

STAR PROFILE
LARRY BIRD

Born: December 7, 1956 West Baden, Indiana

Team: Boston Celtics

Star Stats: 3x NBA champ, 3x NBA MVP

Julius "Dr. J" Erving was an electrifying player. As a forward, his style of play inspired an entire generation of players who followed.

73

GUARDS

There are two guards on the basketball court: a point guard and a shooting guard. But don't let their small size fool you. These players are critical to the teams. And point guards have recorded some of the most impressive statistics in basketball history.

Guard Diana Taurasi of the Phoenix Mercury is a top star in the WNBA. In the 2014 playoffs she scored almost 22 points per game.

Like Mike

Guards are a team's best shooters and passers. They take a lot of shots from outside the **key**. A guard also helps run the team on the floor, much like a quarterback. Also like quarterbacks, guards are often big stars. Michael Jordan, perhaps the NBA's greatest player of all time, was a shooting guard. Jordan led the Chicago Bulls to six championships. He also holds the NBA record for the highest points-per-game average (30.12).

Michael Jordan played guard for the Chicago Bulls and Washington Wizards. He is widely considered the greatest basketball player of all time.

Bob Cousy was one of the great guards from basketball's earlier days. Much of his style carried over to the way guards play the game today.

Great Guards

Just as George Mikan revolutionized the center position, Bob Cousy did the same for guards. He set many assist records during his career and was known for his quick style of play. Earvin "Magic" Johnson was another great point guard. He helped the Lakers to five championships and set playoff assist records in the process. More recently John Stockton showed what a speedy guard can do for his team, setting career assist and steal records.

THE COACH

It takes work to be a good basketball team. The players do their part to improve, and the coach is there to help them. A head coach has a big part in a team's success. No wonder some coaches get almost as much attention as their players.

Coach Pat Summitt explains a play to her team in 2011. Most basketball coaches use a dry-erase board like this during games.

Big Job

A basketball coach has many tasks. He or she prepares the team for its next opponent. This means learning the opponent's strengths and weaknesses. During the game the coach sends in **subs** who best match up against opposing players. The coach even makes sure players are in top shape for long games. The coach usually has one or two assistants to help with all these tasks.

Coach Phil Jackson argues a call with a referee during a game in 2006. Jackson is one of the most successful NBA coaches of all time.

Basketball Brains

John Wooden achieved a coaching record with his UCLA team—it won seven NCAA championships in a row (1967–1973). Pat Summitt was another great coach. She won eight out of every ten games she coached! Another superstar coach is Mike Krzyzewski (pronounced she-SHEV-ski) of Duke University, who had won 1,018 games through the 2014–2015 season. At the pro level, perhaps the greatest coach ever was Phil Jackson. His teams won 11 NBA championships.

In addition to coaching Duke University, Coach Mike Krzyzewski led the USA Olympic basketball team in 2008 and 2012.

THE WNBA

In 1997 a new pro sports league began play in the United States. The Women's National Basketball Association (WNBA) was formed with eight teams. It gives players from women's college basketball a chance to extend their playing careers. It also gives fans exciting basketball action.

Maya Moore of the Minnesota Lynx takes a shot against the Phoenix Mercury. Moore has helped the Lynx win two WNBA championships.

WOW!

On June 2, 2012, Angel McCoughtry of the Atlanta Dream made 17 out of 17 free throw attempts against the Chicago Sky, missing none!

Sue Bird of the Seattle Storm prepares to pass an orange and white WNBA ball. A WNBA ball is 1 inch smaller around than an NBA ball.

WNBA Basics

The WNBA season is held from May to October and lasts 34 games plus playoffs. Game rules are mostly the same as those used in the NBA. One difference is that each quarter is 10 minutes long instead of 12. Since 1997, the league has grown to 12 teams. In addition, WNBA players represent more than 20 nations.

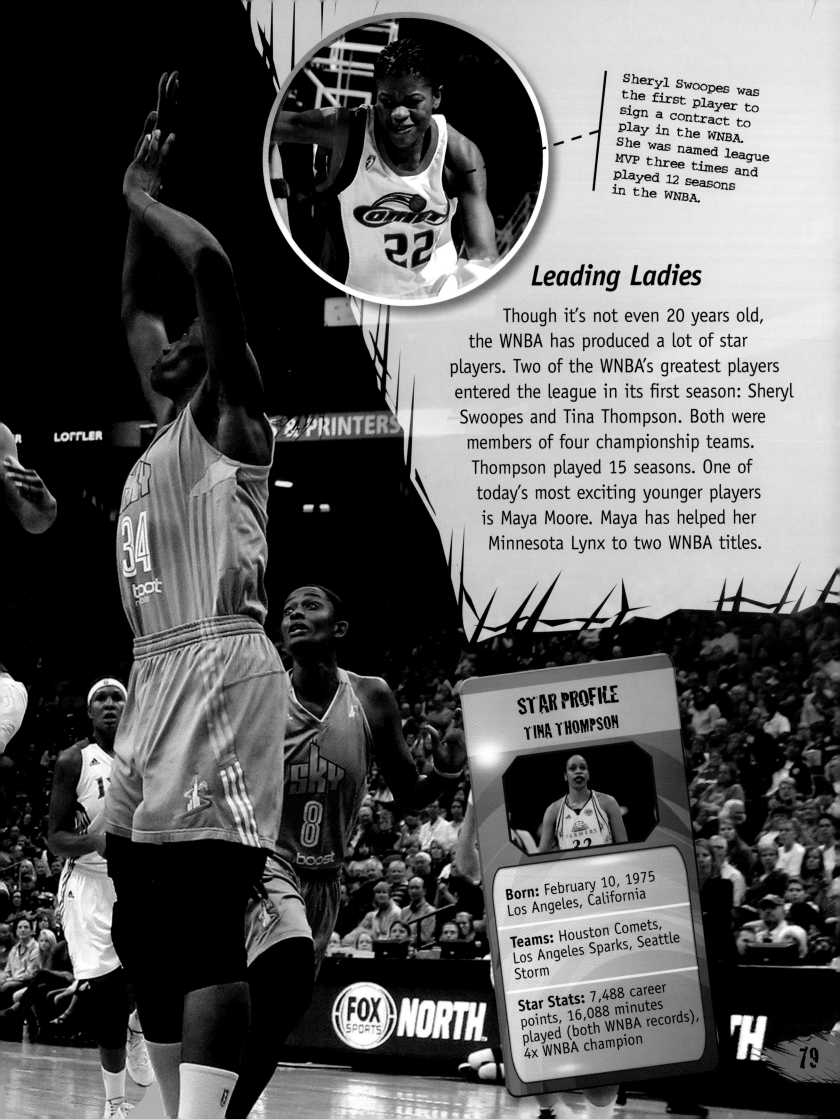

Leading Ladies

Though it's not even 20 years old, the WNBA has produced a lot of star players. Two of the WNBA's greatest players entered the league in its first season: Sheryl Swoopes and Tina Thompson. Both were members of four championship teams. Thompson played 15 seasons. One of today's most exciting younger players is Maya Moore. Maya has helped her Minnesota Lynx to two WNBA titles.

STAR PROFILE
TINA THOMPSON

Born: February 10, 1975 Los Angeles, California

Teams: Houston Comets, Los Angeles Sparks, Seattle Storm

Star Stats: 7,488 career points, 16,088 minutes played (both WNBA records), 4x WNBA champion

MARCH MADNESS

Every spring, basketball fans have something big to cheer about. It's tournament time! The National Collegiate Athletic Association (NCAA) chooses the college teams that will play in the NCAA Tournament. It's the biggest sports story of the month and it's known as "March Madness."

Lew Alcindor led the UCLA Bruins to three NCAA tournaments (1967–1969). As a pro, Alcindor changed his name to Kareem Abdul-Jabbar.

Bracket Basics

Sixty-eight teams are picked to play in the tournament. The teams are placed in a four-part **bracket** and ranked from strongest to weakest. Stronger teams play weaker teams in the first round of games. This is where much of the tournament's excitement comes into play. Every year, some weaker teams upset stronger teams. Before the tournament begins, fans try to predict who will win each game.

STAR PROFILE
CHRISTIAN LAETTNER

Born: August 17, 1969 Angola, New York

Team: Duke University

Star Stats: 407 points, 23 games played (both NCAA Tournament records)

The NCAA Final Four often takes place in football stadiums to hold the huge crowds. Here, Michigan takes on Syracuse at the 2013 Final Four in the Georgia Dome.

An NCAA Tournament bracket has a space for each team. This shows the 64-team bracket used for the women's event. Winners advance to the next round in the bracket until only two teams remain.

From 68 Down to 1

The NCAA Tournament takes more than two weeks to play. With each round, the number of teams decreases by half. The last three rounds are known as the Sweet Sixteen, the Elite Eight, and the Final Four. The Final Four is played at a neutral site. The NCAA also hosts a tournament for its women's teams. The women's event begins with 64 teams.

NBA CHAMPIONSHIP

A few weeks after March Madness, the pros begin their own tournament: the NBA Playoffs. The NBA is considered the world's top basketball league. In the playoffs, the season's best teams compete.

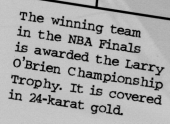

The winning team in the NBA Finals is awarded the Larry O'Brien Championship Trophy. It is covered in 24-karat gold.

How It Works

The 16 NBA teams with the best regular-season records get to play in the **postseason**. The playoffs begin with four best-of-seven series. The first team in each series to win four games moves on to play a new opponent.

Here, the San Antonio Spurs battle the Miami Heat in the 2014 Finals. The Spurs won the series four games to one.

Dynasties

Some teams have enjoyed great playoff success. These teams are known as dynasties. The Boston Celtics and Los Angeles Lakers have had the NBA's most famous dynasties. Other top teams include the Chicago Bulls (1991–1998), Miami Heat (2011–2014), and San Antonio Spurs (1999–2014).

WOW!
The Boston Celtics have won the most NBA Championships (17).

STAR PROFILE
JOE MONTANA

Born: February 12, 1934 West Monroe, Louisiana

Team: Boston Celtics

Star Stats: 11x NBA champion (NBA record)

Scottie Pippen was a small forward who helped the Chicago Bulls win six NBA championships in the 1990s.

Playoff Performers

Every dynasty is powered by great players. Michael Jordan and Scottie Pippen led the Chicago Bulls to six titles in the 1990s. But the player with the most NBA championships is Bill Russell.

SHOOTIN' HOOPS

College and pro basketball players are among the world's most amazing athletes. All of them learned their skills in places like small-town gymnasiums and big-city playgrounds. You can find people of all ages and abilities learning and enjoying basketball across the country.

Outdoor parks are a great place to sharpen your basketball skills.

Youth Leagues

Most players learn basketball rules and skills in youth leagues. These are found at schools, parks, and churches. Often, youth games are played on half courts with lowered nets. This increases scoring chances for younger (and shorter!) players. It also means two games can be played on one court.

Streetball

Public parks are another place to learn basketball. This is sometimes called "streetball" because the courts are outdoors and made of asphalt, just like a street. Older, more skilled players can also be found playing at parks. Some of the best NBA players learned the game and sharpened their skills here.

Streetball tournaments can attract great amateur players—as well as a lot of fans—in cities around the world.

More than 100,000 people around the world compete in wheelchair basketball. It can be played outdoors or on a standard basketball court.

Friends play a game of one-on-one at an outdoor park. Nearly every town and city in the USA has at least one park with a backboard and net.

Get Out and Play

One of the best things about basketball is that just two people can play. Grab a friend at the park for a game of **horse** or **one-on-one**. Both are fantastic ways to practice dribbling and shooting—and to get exercise and hang out with a friend!

HOCKEY

Watch a game of hockey and right away you'll notice that something is very different. This sport is played on ice and the players wear skates on their feet! It might be a strange sport to a newcomer, but hockey has a long history. Plus, each year more and more people try it out. Let's learn more about this fast game's gear, rules, and greatest players past and present.

A hockey arena can be a small metal building with just a few wooden benches, or a large building that holds thousands of fans, like this arena in Quebec, Canada.

HOCKEY HISTORY

Hockey's history is rooted in sports from other cultures. Some of these sports were brought to the USA and Canada from Europe. In North America they were combined with games played by Native Americans. As with baseball and football, new rules developed. This led to hockey as we now know it.

Shinty or Shinney?

Two sports from which hockey grew came from very different cultures but share similar names. Shinty is a game played on grass in Scotland. It's been around for more than 2,000 years. Players use curved sticks to shoot a ball into the other team's net. Shinney was a similar stick-and-ball game played by some Native American tribes on huge fields. Today, informal ice hockey played outdoors is known as shinny (with no "e").

Hockey grew from other sports, such as the Scottish game of shinty.

Hockey Is Born

Other sports that were brought to North America included shinty-like games played on skates on rivers in England and the Netherlands. The first indoor game that resembled hockey as we now know it was played in Montreal, Quebec, Canada on March 3, 1875. By 1900 there were hundreds of teams across Canada. Hockey has long been known as Canada's sport, much as baseball is America's pastime.

Men play ice hockey in Chamonix in the French Alps about 1900.

Many cultures around the world have enjoyed hockey-like sports. This 19th-century engraving shows indigenous people in Chile playing a game called cineca.

WOW!

Hockey players can get going pretty fast on their skates—around 30 miles per hour!

FACEOFF

LEFT WING

Hockey's ice is called a rink. The rink is surrounded by a wall, or "boards," to keep the puck in play. Most rinks are inside arenas. But hockey is especially popular in areas that have cold winters. There, players enjoy extra ice time on outdoor rinks.

FACEOFF CIRCLE

GOALIE

NET

DEFENSEMEN

The Parts of a Rink

In the USA and Canada, most rinks from the youth level to the National Hockey League (NHL) are 200 feet long and 85 feet wide. The middle of the rink, between two blue lines, is the neutral zone. The area from a blue line to the end of the rink is the offensive zone. The rink also has nine faceoff circles. Here, a referee drops the puck between two players to start the action.

A hockey net is made of red steel pipes and nylon mesh. Its opening is 6 feet wide and 4 feet tall

A hockey team has six players on the ice, including one goalie. These children in Moscow, Russia, are playing a game on a half-rink.

WOW!

It takes up to 15,000 gallons of water to create a hockey rink measuring 200 feet by 85 feet!

CENTER

When a hockey player breaks a rule, he or she must sit in the penalty box for two or even five minutes. This means their team is a player short.

Pass and Shoot

Hockey games are split into three periods. Each team has six players on the ice. They move the puck by passing it to each other. They try to score goals by shooting the puck past their opponents' goalie and into the net. But the other team might suddenly regain control of the puck. The team that was trying to score must quickly switch to playing defense and prevent their opponent from scoring.

HOCKEY EQUIPMENT

HELMET

MASK

SHOULDER PADS

Hockey is a sport with a lot of contact. The players carry sticks and shoot a hard puck. Players at older levels are allowed to **check** each other to get control of the puck. Players must wear special equipment.

GLOVES

STICK

Hockey is fast and has lots of contact. Players wear gear that protects them.

PUCK

WOW!

Some NHL players go through more than 100 sticks in a single season. NHL teams spend several hundred thousand dollars on sticks each year.

Skates, Stick, and Puck

For a friendly game of hockey you need three things besides ice: skates, a hockey stick, and a puck. Skates have a leather boot and a sharp steel blade. The blade cuts into the ice so that the player does not slip around. The long L-shaped stick has a blade, too, but it is not sharp. It is used to **stickhandle**, pass, and shoot the puck. The puck is made of hard rubber and weighs six ounces.

A player laces up her skates before a game. Skates are kept sharp with a round, spinning stone that grinds a new edge onto the metal blades.

ELBOW PADS

JERSEY

BREEZERS

SKATES

SHIN PADS

SOCKS

Staying Safe

In games and practices, players wear protective gear. Shin, shoulder, and elbow pads, as well as gloves, are made of dense foam and plastic. Breezers cover the thighs, hips, kidneys, and tailbone. Finally, players at all levels must wear a rugged helmet. Wire masks on younger players' helmets protect their faces from pucks and sticks.

The helmet is an important piece of hockey gear. Kids must also wear a wire mask like this one. Helmets didn't become the rule in the NHL until 1979.

THE GOALIE

CHEST AND ARM
PROTECTORS
UNDER JERSEY

MASK

There are five positions on a hockey team. The skater positions are center, left and right wing, and two defensive players. The fifth position is goalie. He or she must stop the puck when opponents try to score.

Carey Price is one of the top goalies in the NHL. Check out his equipment!

BLOCKER

Lots of Protection

Goalies wear more protection than their teammates. Hockey pucks are rock hard and travel at high speeds. A mask shields the head and face. Chest, arm, and leg pads cover the body. The skates have thick plastic toe caps. Finally, a goalie wears special gloves—a blocker on the hand that holds the stick and a trapper mitt on the hand that catches pucks. When the goalie stops the puck, it's called a save. A goalie who allows no goals in a game earns a shutout.

STICK

In 1960 Jacques Plante became the first NHL goalie to regularly wear a mask. He went on to design masks for other goalies, too.

TRAPPER MITT

LEG PADS

GOALIE SKATES

Legend of the Crease

The blue area in front of a hockey net is called the crease. Skaters are not allowed in this area. Georges Vezina was one of the early greats to patrol the crease. He played 16 seasons for the Montreal Canadiens (1910–1926). The trophy given to NHL's best goalie is named after him.

Goalies are famous for their superstitions! Patrick Roy once claimed that he talked to his net's metal posts during games.

STAR PROFILE
MARTIN BRODEUR

Born: May 6, 1972
Montreal, Quebec, Canada

Teams: New Jersey Devils, St. Louis Blues

Star Stats: 1,471 total games played (1,260 regular-season games and 205 playoffs), 804 wins, and 149 shutouts

THE CENTER

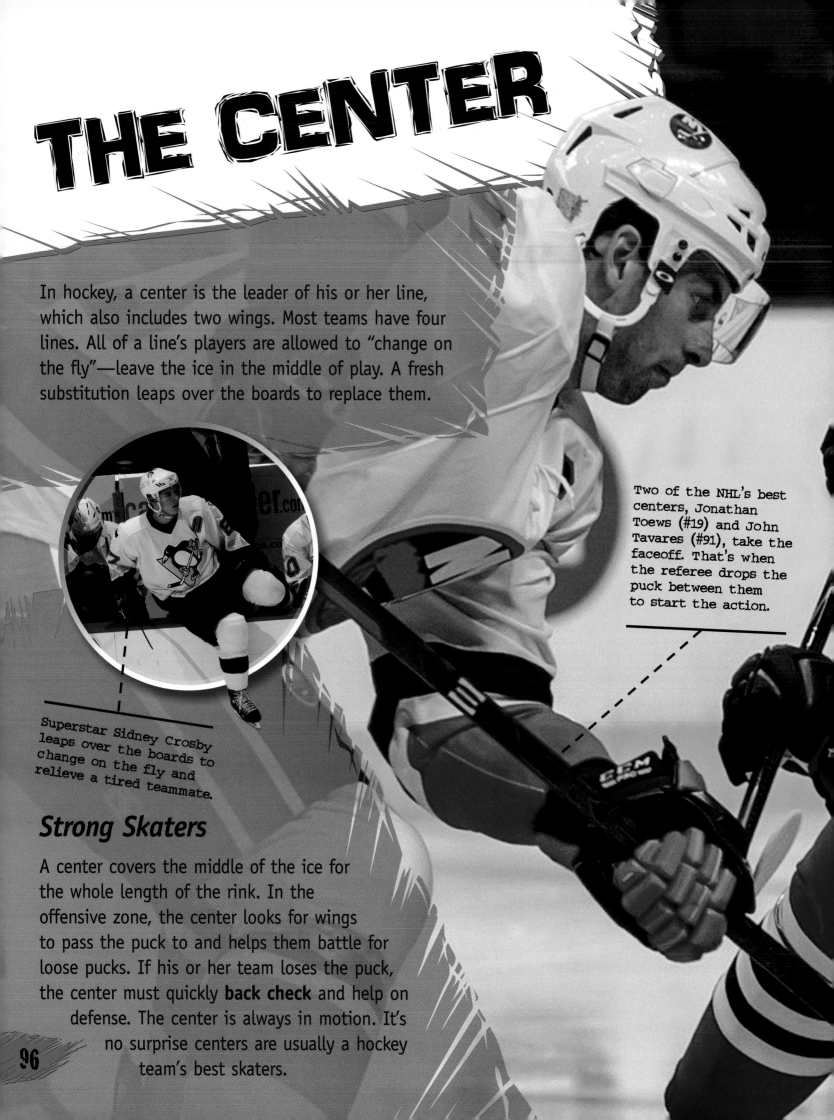

In hockey, a center is the leader of his or her line, which also includes two wings. Most teams have four lines. All of a line's players are allowed to "change on the fly"—leave the ice in the middle of play. A fresh substitution leaps over the boards to replace them.

Two of the NHL's best centers, Jonathan Toews (#19) and John Tavares (#91), take the faceoff. That's when the referee drops the puck between them to start the action.

Superstar Sidney Crosby leaps over the boards to change on the fly and relieve a tired teammate.

Strong Skaters

A center covers the middle of the ice for the whole length of the rink. In the offensive zone, the center looks for wings to pass the puck to and helps them battle for loose pucks. If his or her team loses the puck, the center must quickly **back check** and help on defense. The center is always in motion. It's no surprise centers are usually a hockey team's best skaters.

Superstar Centers

Two of the NHL's best players were centers. Mario Lemieux played 17 seasons (1984–1997, 2000–2006). He racked up 766 goals and 1,129 assists. Another center, Wayne Gretzky, is considered by many to be the finest hockey player ever. Known as "the Great One," he holds 60 NHL records. Today's biggest NHL star is Sidney Crosby, a center for the Pittsburgh Penguins.

Wayne Gretzky played 21 NHL seasons. He's still the only player to record 200 points in one season— and he did it four times!

STAR PROFILE
WAYNE GRETZKY

Born: January 26, 1961 Brantford, Ontario, Canada

Teams: Edmonton Oilers, Los Angeles Kings, St. Louis Blues, New York Rangers

Star Stats: 1,016 career goals, 2,345 career assists (both NHL records) . . . plus 58 other NHL records!

WOW!
Joe Malone of the old Quebec Bulldogs holds the record for scoring the most goals in one game. He scored seven on January 31, 1920.

WINGS

The wings are the center's linemates. One wing plays on each side of the center: a left wing and right wing. Together, these three are the players most responsible for creating scoring chances.

Left wing Alexander Ovechkin of Russia (in white) battles two US opponents for the puck during the 2014 World Championships.

Winger Patrick Kane of the Chicago Blackhawks often represents Team USA in international competition.

Puck Control

When the puck goes into the opponents' zone, a wing tries to get to it before an opponent. The other wing might go to the **slot** in front of the net and wait for a pass. Wings also check opponents to gain control of the puck. Like the center, wings must get back and help out on defense too.

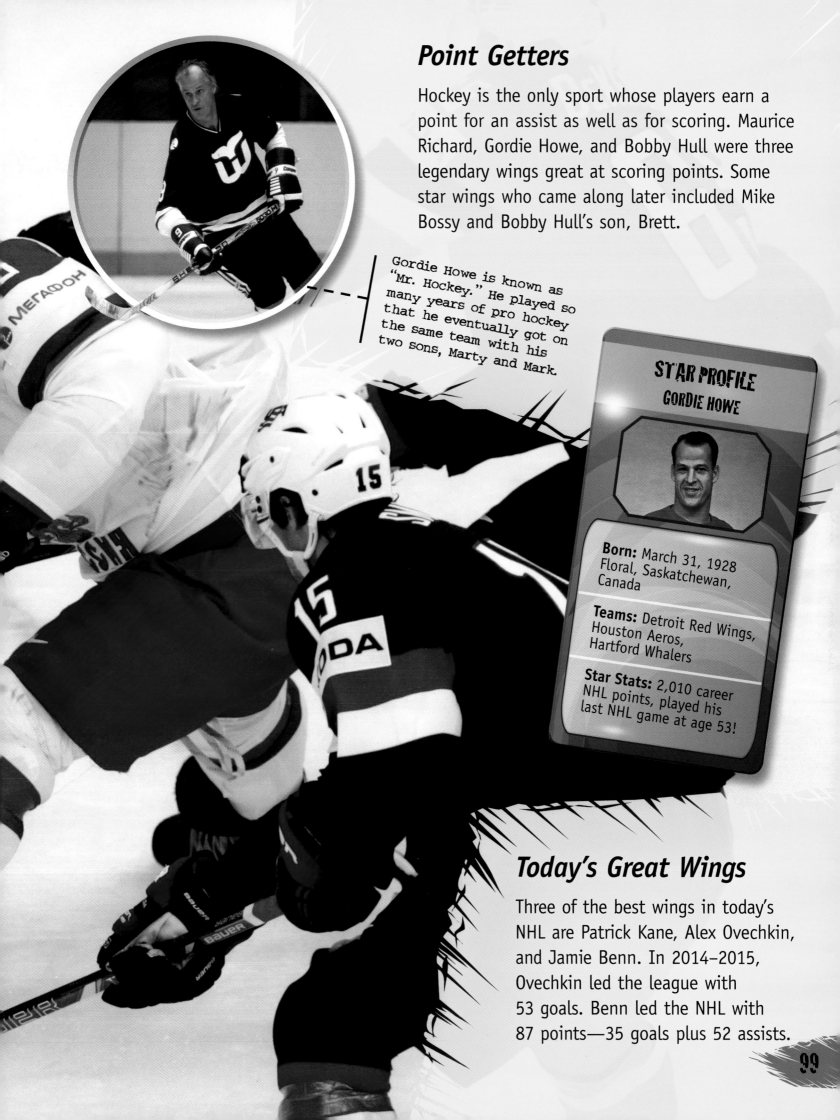

Point Getters

Hockey is the only sport whose players earn a point for an assist as well as for scoring. Maurice Richard, Gordie Howe, and Bobby Hull were three legendary wings great at scoring points. Some star wings who came along later included Mike Bossy and Bobby Hull's son, Brett.

Gordie Howe is known as "Mr. Hockey." He played so many years of pro hockey that he eventually got on the same team with his two sons, Marty and Mark.

STAR PROFILE
GORDIE HOWE

Born: March 31, 1928 Floral, Saskatchewan, Canada

Teams: Detroit Red Wings, Houston Aeros, Hartford Whalers

Star Stats: 2,010 career NHL points, played his last NHL game at age 53!

Today's Great Wings

Three of the best wings in today's NHL are Patrick Kane, Alex Ovechkin, and Jamie Benn. In 2014–2015, Ovechkin led the league with 53 goals. Benn led the NHL with 87 points—35 goals plus 52 assists.

DEFENSEMEN

Two defensemen are on the ice with the center and wings. Defensemen can score goals and assists, too. Their main job, however, is to prevent the other team's wings and centers from taking shots at their team's net.

WOW!

At 6 feet 9 inches, defenseman Zdeno Chara is the tallest player in NHL history.

Big Blueliners

When the puck enters their zone, one defenseman must get to it first. Defensemen move the puck out of their zone with sharp passes to the center or a wing. When the puck is in the offensive zone, defensemen stand just inside the blue line. If the puck comes to them they keep it in the zone. Sometimes they do this with a **slap shot** at the opposing team's net.

Zdeno Chara of the Boston Bruins holds the record for the fastest slap shot at 108.8 miles per hour.

Thanks to Orr

Bobby Orr changed the way defensemen play hockey. He entered the NHL in 1966–1967 at 18 years old. Orr showed that defensemen can skate with the puck and create scoring chances, too. Thanks to Orr, talented young defensemen like Ottawa Senator Erik Karlsson and Montreal Canadien P. K. Subban are scoring threats as well as solid defenders.

Many believe Bobby Orr was the greatest defenseman ever. He proved that a player at his position could be an offensive threat too.

STAR PROFILE
BOBBY ORR

Born: March 20, 1948 Parry Sound, Ontario, Canada

Teams: Boston Bruins, Chicago Black Hawks

Star Stats: 102 assists, 139 points in 1970–1971 (single-season NHL records for a defenseman)

Minnesota Wild defenseman Ryan Suter takes a slap shot at the opposing team's net. Suter averaged more than 29 minutes of ice time per NHL game in 2014–2015.

THE COACH

A hockey coach is often called the person "behind the bench." This refers to the place where coaches stand during a game. NHL coaches are under a great deal of pressure. If their team doesn't make the playoffs, they might find themselves without a job!

Chicago Blackhawks coach Joel Quenneville seems unhappy with a referee. "Coach Q" has the most career wins of any current NHL coach: 754 through the 2014–2015 regular season.

Detroit Red Wings coach Mike Babcock instructs his players during the 2014 Winter Classic, an NHL game played outdoors each year.

Brain behind the Bench

Head coaches choose their team's **roster**. They also decide what strategies their team will use throughout the season. They hold practice sessions for their team almost every day—even before games. During a game, the coach changes the team's lines to give players the best matchup against their opponents. Luckily, coaches usually have several assistant coaches to help them.

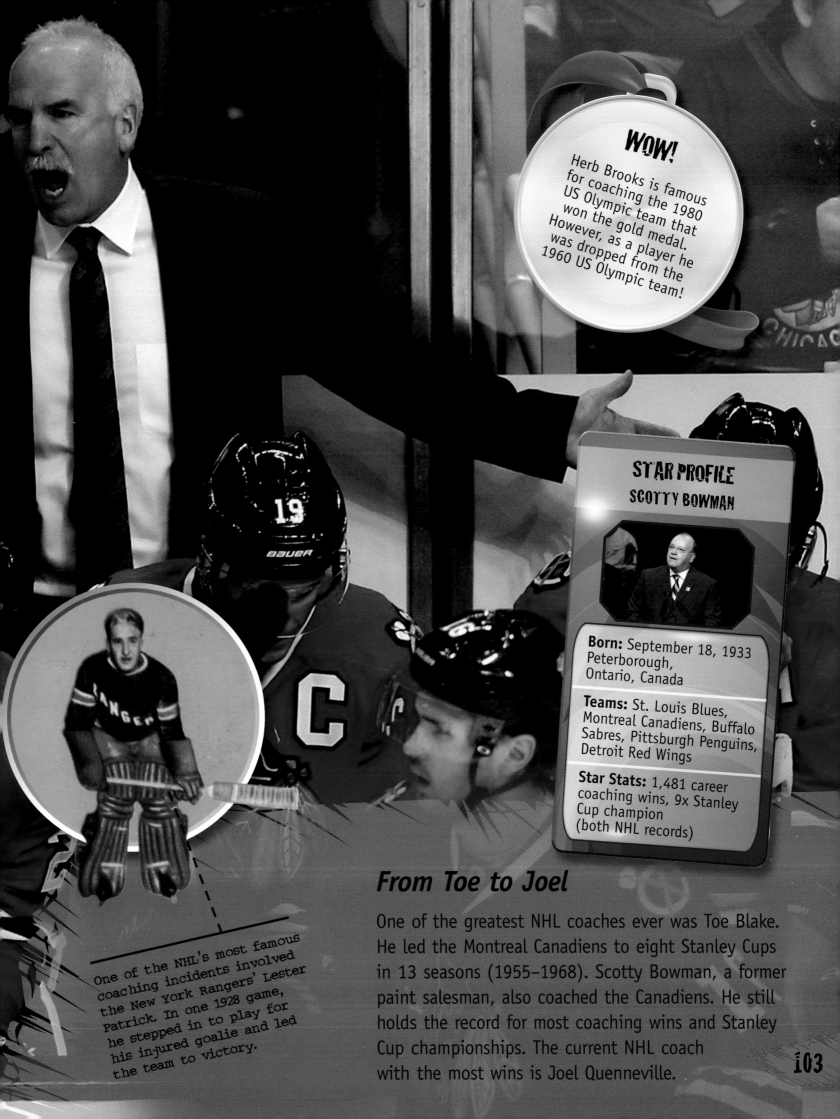

STAR PROFILE

SCOTTY BOWMAN

Born: September 18, 1933
Peterborough,
Ontario, Canada

Teams: St. Louis Blues,
Montreal Canadiens, Buffalo
Sabres, Pittsburgh Penguins,
Detroit Red Wings

Star Stats: 1,481 career
coaching wins, 9x Stanley
Cup champion
(both NHL records)

One of the NHL's most famous coaching incidents involved the New York Rangers' Lester Patrick. In one 1928 game, he stepped in to play for his injured goalie and led the team to victory.

From Toe to Joel

One of the greatest NHL coaches ever was Toe Blake. He led the Montreal Canadiens to eight Stanley Cups in 13 seasons (1955–1968). Scotty Bowman, a former paint salesman, also coached the Canadiens. He still holds the record for most coaching wins and Stanley Cup championships. The current NHL coach with the most wins is Joel Quenneville.

103

WOMEN'S HOCKEY

Women's hockey teams have been around since the 1800s. In the last 20 years, however, women's and girls' hockey has become popular at the youth, college, and professional levels. Today, 88 US colleges and universities have women's hockey teams. In Canada there are 30 university teams.

Most girls learn hockey basics by playing and practicing with boys. As they get older, girls join their own leagues.

The Basics

The rules of women's hockey are mostly the same as the rules for the men's game. The major difference is that body checking is not allowed in women's hockey. Like boys, girls can begin playing hockey at an early age. At the youngest levels it is common for boys and girls to learn the game's basic skills together.

Many colleges and universities in the northern half of the USA have women's hockey teams. Here, the Boston College Eagles' Haley Skarupa skates past two Cornell University forwards.

College Powerhouses

Organized women's hockey has not been around as long as men's hockey. However, the sport has still produced awesome players and teams, especially at the college level. Some schools have had women's teams since the 1960s, but the NCAA women's hockey tournament only began in 2001. In 15 years, the University of Minnesota and the University of Minnesota–Duluth have both won five championships.

The Minnesota Golden Gophers are one of the best women's college teams in the US.

WOW!
The University of Minnesota Golden Gophers women's team won 62 straight games from February 2012 to November 2013. That's a record for both men's and women's hockey.

STAR PROFILE
CAMMI GRANATO

Born: March 25, 1971 Downers Grove, Illinois

Teams: Providence College, McGill University, Team USA

Star Stats: 1x Olympic gold medalist (1998), 1x Olympic silver medalist (2002), one of the first two women inducted into the Hockey Hall of Fame

INTERNATIONAL HOCKEY

Hockey has been popular in Canada and the northern USA for more than a century. But did you know it's a very popular sport in other nations too? According to the NHL, 33 percent of its players are now from Europe. And more and more European players are joining college teams in the USA and junior teams in Canada.

WOW!

Russia (formerly the Soviet Union) has won 27 World Championships gold medals versus Canada's 24. From 1963 to 1990, the Soviets won 20 of 25 world titles.

Some NHL players get the chance to play for their countries at international tournaments. Here Finland take on their rival Sweden in 2014.

The Big Four

The biggest hockey countries in Europe are Sweden, Finland, Russia, and the Czech Republic. The sport is also popular in Switzerland, Austria, Norway, Germany, Slovakia, and elsewhere. The International Ice Hockey Federation (IIHF) even hosts international tournaments for nations with developing hockey programs. Today, 56 countries have national teams.

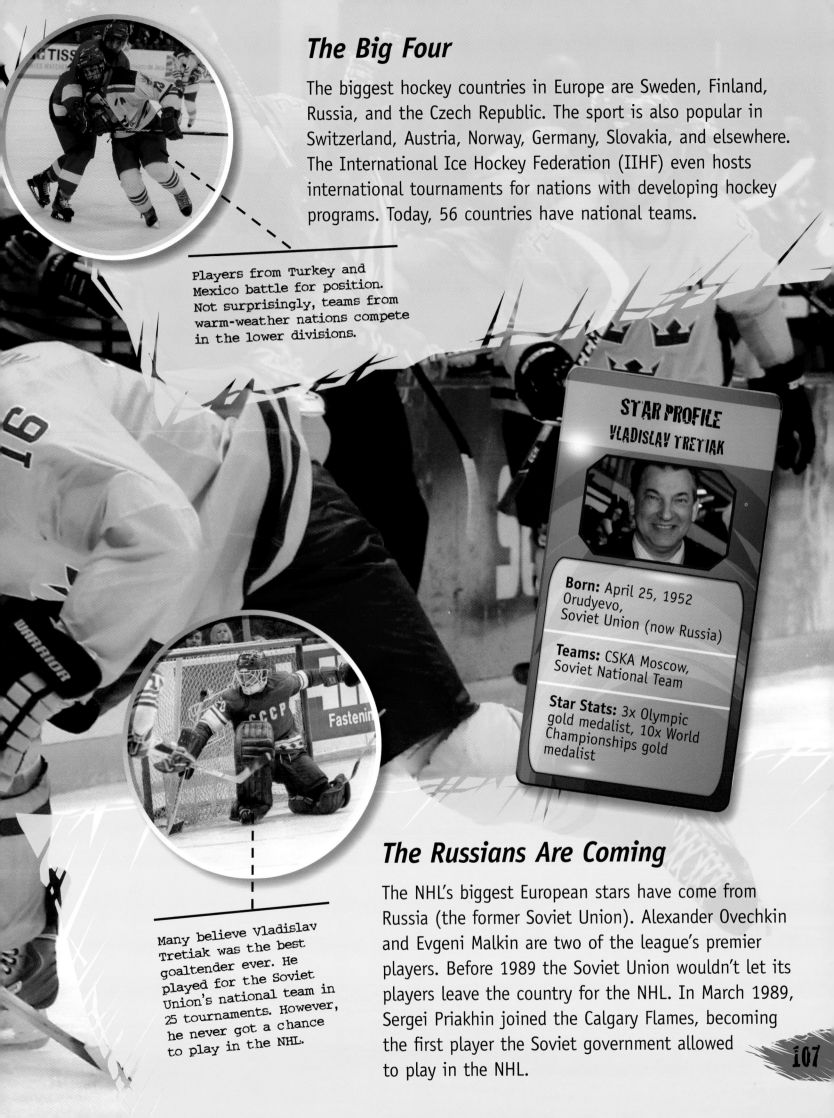

Players from Turkey and Mexico battle for position. Not surprisingly, teams from warm-weather nations compete in the lower divisions.

STAR PROFILE
VLADISLAV TRETIAK

Born: April 25, 1952 Orudyevo, Soviet Union (now Russia)

Teams: CSKA Moscow, Soviet National Team

Star Stats: 3x Olympic gold medalist, 10x World Championships gold medalist

Many believe Vladislav Tretiak was the best goaltender ever. He played for the Soviet Union's national team in 25 tournaments. However, he never got a chance to play in the NHL.

The Russians Are Coming

The NHL's biggest European stars have come from Russia (the former Soviet Union). Alexander Ovechkin and Evgeni Malkin are two of the league's premier players. Before 1989 the Soviet Union wouldn't let its players leave the country for the NHL. In March 1989, Sergei Priakhin joined the Calgary Flames, becoming the first player the Soviet government allowed to play in the NHL.

THE STANLEY CUP

Hockey's greatest prize is the Stanley Cup. It's the oldest pro sports trophy in North America. Each year, 30 NHL teams begin the season hoping they'll be the ones to lift the cup at season's end. Only one team can win—that's what makes the Stanley Cup so special.

WOW!

As of 2014, the Stanley Cup had 3,073 names engraved on it—and 14 of those had been misspelled!

Lord of the Rings

The Stanley Cup is named for Lord Stanley of Preston, the former governor of Canada. He had the trophy made to give to Canada's top **amateur** hockey club each year. In 1915 Canada's pro teams took over the cup. The Stanley Cup is much taller now than when it was first made. That is because rings have been added at the bottom, engraved with the names of players in the winning teams.

Each ring holds the names from 13 teams. The bowl at the top is a replica of the one donated by Lord Stanley in 1892

STAR PROFILE
HENRI RICHARD

Born: February 29, 1936
Montreal, Quebec, Canada

Team: Montreal Canadiens

Star Stats: 11x Stanley Cup champion (NHL record)

Cup Traditions

Since the Stanley Cup was first won in 1893, many traditions have grown around it. After the cup is awarded to the captain of the winning team, each player takes a turn skating it around the rink. What's more, each player gets to spend a day with the cup—no matter where they live. The Stanley Cup has traveled more than 1,000,000 miles in the last ten years!

Patrice Bergeron of the Boston Bruins raised the Stanley Cup after the Bruins won it in 2011.

Competition for the Stanley Cup is fierce. Here, the Vancouver Canucks celebrate winning against the San Jose Sharks and advancing to the 2011 Stanley Cup Finals.

DROP THE PUCK!

Hockey is famous for its speed and intense competition. But the best thing about the sport is that it's fun. You don't have to be a pro to get in on it. Sometimes you don't even need ice!

Hockey is very popular in many cold-weather areas. These two boys are taking a break from a game of shinny on their backyard rink.

Rink Rats

Hockey can be addictive. People who hang out at ice rinks all day are called "rink rats." During the winter, some even build backyard rinks so they can skate whenever they want. In colder areas, public parks sometimes have outdoor rinks with skates and sticks you can use. And some NHL teams host "Learn to Play Hockey" days. You can try on gear, hit the ice, and find out if hockey's for you.

Sled hockey is played by athletes who are unable to walk. Players use two short sticks to move themselves around the ice and to shoot the puck.

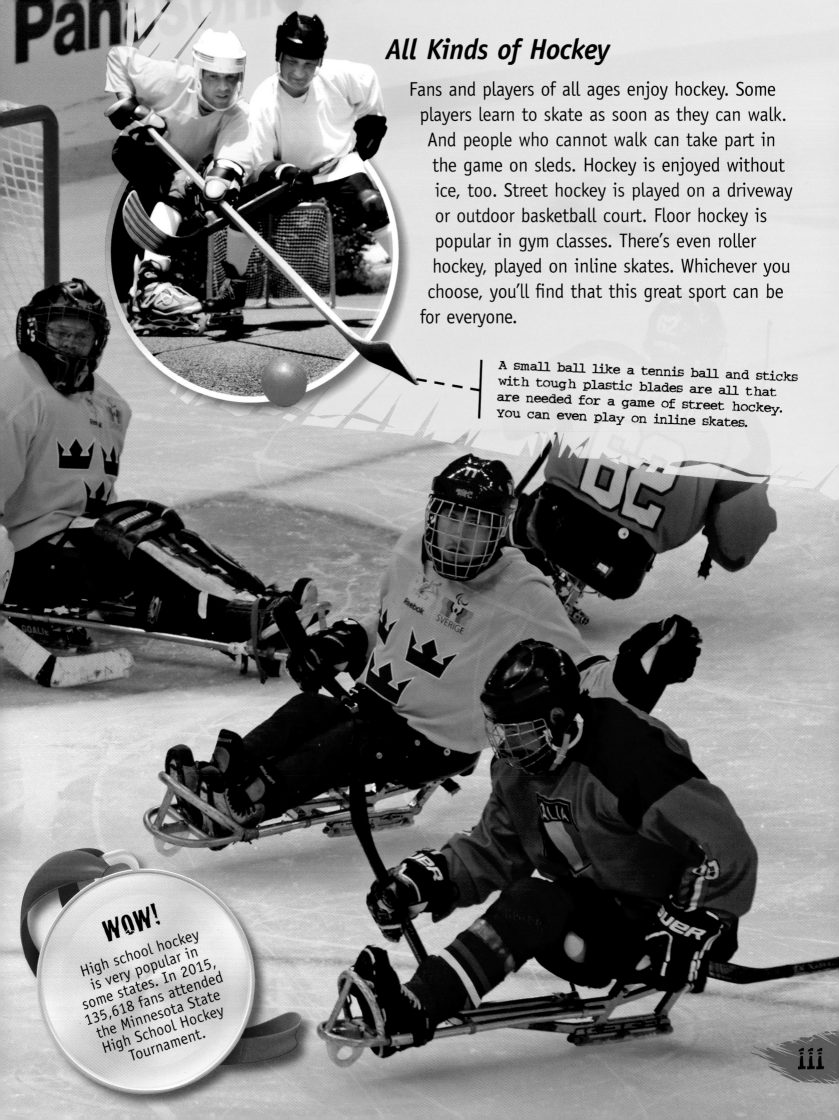

All Kinds of Hockey

Fans and players of all ages enjoy hockey. Some players learn to skate as soon as they can walk. And people who cannot walk can take part in the game on sleds. Hockey is enjoyed without ice, too. Street hockey is played on a driveway or outdoor basketball court. Floor hockey is popular in gym classes. There's even roller hockey, played on inline skates. Whichever you choose, you'll find that this great sport can be for everyone.

A small ball like a tennis ball and sticks with tough plastic blades are all that are needed for a game of street hockey. You can even play on inline skates.

WOW!
High school hockey is very popular in some states. In 2015, 135,618 fans attended the Minnesota State High School Hockey Tournament.

OLYMPIC SPORTS

Every four years millions of people gather in a single city to watch the world's greatest sporting event: the Olympic Games. The modern Olympics began in 1896 with just a few sports. Today's games feature dozens of sports. Since 1924 there has also been a separate Winter Olympics. Let's take a look at some of the more popular sports, athletes, and records of the Summer and Winter Olympics.

Spectators wave flags in the Olympic Stadium at the 2012 Summer Olympics, which was held in London, UK.

WOW!

The original Olympics were held more than 2,700 years ago in Olympia, ancient Greece, to honor Zeus, king of the gods.

TRACK AND FIELD

Foot races, the long jump, and the discus were all featured in the ancient Greek games. Today, track and field (sometimes called "athletics") is as popular in the Summer Olympics as it was 2,700 years ago.

Need for Speed

Running sports are the main track and field events. The shortest (and speediest) are the sprints. Runners burst from starting blocks for races measuring 100, 200, and 400 meters. Sprints also include 4x100 and 4x200 relay races. The hurdles are also short but fast. These events measure 110 meters (100 meters for women) and 400 meters. Athletes leap over fence-like obstacles. The men's Olympic record in the 400-meter hurdles (46.78 seconds) is also a world record.

The success of US athlete Jesse Owens at the 1936 Olympics in Germany embarrassed German officials. They believed that white athletes were unbeatable.

Going the Distance

Olympic track and field includes longer races of 1,500, 5,000, and 10,000 meters (roughly 1, 3, and 6 miles). In the 3,000-meter steeplechase (a little less than 2 miles) runners leap over obstacles called steeples. On the other side, a shallow pool of water awaits them! The longest Olympic foot race is the marathon. At 26.2 miles, it takes more than two hours to complete. The Olympic marathon records are 2:06:32 for men and 2:23:07 for women.

Usain Bolt of Jamaica holds the Olympic record in the 100 meters. He won the gold medal in 2012 with a time of 9.63 seconds.

Unlike other running events, which are held on a stadium track, the marathon takes place on city streets.

WOW!

Finnish runner Paavo Nurmi owns the record for most track and field medals in the Olympics—nine gold and three silver!

STAR PROFILE
JESSE OWENS

Born: September 12, 1913 Oakville, Alabama
Died: March 31, 1980

Sports: Sprints, long jump

Olympic Record: 4x gold medalist for 100 meters, 200 meters, long jump, 4x100 meter relay (1936)

FIELD EVENTS

The foot races are the "track" part of "track and field." A number of other interesting contests are held in the area inside the running track. These are called the field events.

WOW!

The men's Olympic record throw for the discus is 69.89 meters (229.3 feet), set in 2004. The women's record is 72.30 meters (237.2 feet), set in 1988.

Throwing Things

Some field events involve the athletes throwing objects. The shot is a heavy ball, usually made of metal, and the javelin is a long spear. The discus is a flat, plate-like object, and the hammer is a heavy ball attached to a wire. In the discus and hammer throws, athletes spin around several times before releasing the object.

This is US shot putter Michelle Carter. She releases the shot in a striking motion, almost like throwing a punch.

A pole vaulter's long, flexible pole propels them up and over the high bar, kind of like a catapult. They land on a soft, air-filled mattress.

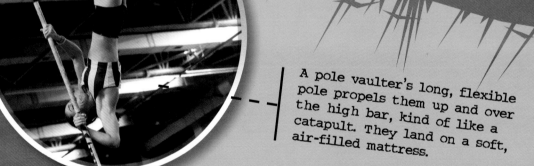

Long jumpers take a running start of about twenty strides. The women's Olympic long jump record is 7.4 meters (24 feet, 3 inches).

Jumping and Vaulting

In the long jump and triple jump, contestants dash down a runway before leaping as far as they can. A pit of sand softens their landing. Foam and air mattresses soften landings for high jumpers and pole vaulters. High jumpers leap over a bar almost 8 feet off the ground. Pole vaulters use a long pole to propel themselves even higher—18 feet or more!

GYMNASTICS

Gymnasts are athletes who combine strength, coordination, and artistry. They compete in several Olympic events. These are usually described as rhythmic and artistic gymnastics. Gymnastic performances are rated by judges from various nations.

The World Rhythmic Gymnastics Championships, shown here, began in 1963. The sport became part of the Olympics in 1984.

Rhythmic Routines

Only women compete in rhythmic gymnastics. They perform **routines** set to music that they choose. They also use one of four kinds of **apparatus** in their routine—a ball, clubs, a hoop, or a long ribbon—which they twirl, toss, and catch. The gymnasts wear thin slippers and perform on a large mat. They can compete alone and in teams of six.

The ribbon is just one apparatus used in rhythmic gymnastics. The ribbon is attached to a stick and must be at least 20 feet long.

Artistic Gymnastics

Artistic gymnastics stars both men and women. The men perform routines on the floor and on five apparatuses: the horizontal bar, parallel bars, pommel horse, rings, and vault. Women also have a floor exercise and vault. In addition there are women's events for the balance beam and uneven parallel bars. The goal in both types of gymnastics is to perform skills as perfectly as possible—and to make it look easy!

Italian gymnast Alberto Busnari performs artistic gymnastics on the pommel horse.

WATER SPORTS

A lot of people enjoy going to the pool or lake on a hot summer day. It's fitting that the Summer Olympics feature water sports. But these athletes aren't out for a fun swim. This is intense competition!

STAR PROFILE
MICHAEL PHELPS

Born: June 30, 1985
Towson, Maryland

Sport: Swimming (backstroke, butterfly, freestyle, individual medley relay)

Olympic Record: 22 Olympic medals, including 18 golds (2004, 2008, 2012)

Swimming Styles

Olympic swimming consists of 17 races for men and women. Swimmers compete in freestyle, backstroke, butterfly, and breaststroke. Races range from 50 meters (164 feet) to 10 kilometers (6.2 miles!). Swimming also has relay races. In the 4x100-meter medley relay, each team member swims a different **stroke.**

Most swimmers wear goggles to help them see and swim caps to prevent their hair from slowing them down through the water.

Water Polo

In water polo two teams try to score by throwing a ball into their opponents' goal. Players must swim or **tread water** without touching the bottom with their feet during the entire match—and matches have four eight-minute periods! Each squad has seven players who wear caps so they can tell their teammates from opponents.

Water polo players are excellent swimmers.

Synchronized swimming is another aquatic sport at the Olympics. The routines are scored by a panel of judges.

Diving

There is springboard and platform diving at the Olympics. In springboard events, athletes dive from a long, flexible board 3 meters (10 feet, 10 inches) above the water. Platform divers leap from a solid surface 10 meters (32 feet, 10 inches) high. Divers are judged on their form and the difficulty of their dives.

WOW!

Divers in 10-meter platform competitions hit the water at up to 35 miles per hour.

RACKET SPORTS

Racket sports come in many varieties. Three of them featured in the Summer Olympics: tennis, table tennis, and badminton.

Sabine Lisicki and Christopher Kas of Germany compete in mixed doubles tennis at the 2012 Olympics.

Venus and Serena Williams celebrate their gold-medal win in doubles tennis at the 2008 Olympics.

Top Tennis

Today, the world's best pro players represent their countries in Olympic tennis. Matches are played on a 78-foot-long court. Courts may have hard (asphalt), clay, or grass surfaces. The Olympics host both singles (one-on-one) and doubles (two-on-two) matches.

STAR PROFILE
VENUS AND SERENA WILLIAMS

Born: June 17, 1980, and September 26, 1981 Lynwood, California and Saginaw, Michigan

Sports: Women's singles and doubles tennis

Olympic Record: 3 gold medals for doubles (2000, 2008, 2012), 1 gold each for singles (2008, 2012)

122

Olympic Ping-Pong

Table tennis is better known as Ping-Pong. At the Olympic level, players have super hand-eye coordination. The ball is only 1.5 inches wide, but players hit it up to 70 miles per hour on a table measuring just 9 feet by 5 feet. The first player or doubles team to score 21 points wins the set. The first to win two sets takes the match.

WOW!

Chinese players have won 47 of the 88 Olympic medals awarded at table tennis since 1988.

Ding Ning of China won a silver medal in women's table tennis at the 2012 Olympics.

A badminton mixed doubles team swats the birdie back over the net.

Bye, Bye, Birdie

Badminton is a fast-paced sport first played at the Olympics in 1992. Players use rackets with long handles to swat a **shuttlecock,** or "birdie," over a net set 5 feet above the court. The object is similar to tennis and table tennis. Athletes compete in singles, doubles, and **mixed doubles**.

TEAM SPORTS

From cycling to swimming to gymnastics, many Olympic sports focus on individual performances. But team sports are an important part of the Games too. Here are a few.

Super Soccer

Men's soccer has been a part of the modern Olympic Games since 1900. Women's soccer was only added in 1996. Sixteen teams play in both the men's and women's tournaments. Outside the United States, soccer is better known as football, the name it is played under at the Olympics.

STAR PROFILE
CRISTIANE

Born: May 15, 1985
Sao Paulo, Brazil

Sport: Soccer

Olympic Record: 12 total goals (2004, 2008, 2012)

Tobin Heath has earned two Olympic gold medals with the USA women's soccer team (2008 and 2012). Here, she and Team USA are taking on China in a 2013 tournament.

Team USA's Jacob Gibb dives for a ball in a beach volleyball match at the 2012 Olympics while his teammate, Sean Rosenthal, looks on.

Field Hockey

The idea of field hockey is similar to that of ice hockey: score goals in your opponents' net. Field hockey teams have 11 players and the game is played on a 100-yard-long grass field, or "pitch." The teams use a hard ball instead of a puck.

Field hockey has been a part of the Olympics for men since 1908 and for women since 1980.

Handy Ball Game

Like racket sports, volleyball is played on a court divided by a net. Unlike racket sports, players use their hands to hit the ball over the net. Indoors, teams of six players compete against each other. In 1996 beach volleyball was added to the Summer Olympics. In this sport, two-player teams compete outdoors on a sand court.

COMBAT SPORTS

In combat sports athletes compete one-on-one in contests of intense physical contact. They are divided into weight classes to help make the matches fair.

The focus of taekwondo is kicking. Athletes wear protective gear on their bodies and heads.

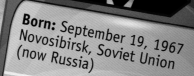

STAR PROFILE
ALEKSANDR KARELIN

Born: September 19, 1967 Novosibirsk, Soviet Union (now Russia)

Sport: Greco-Roman wrestling

Olympic Record: 3x gold, 1x silver medalist (1988, 1992, 1996, 2000)

World-Class Wrestling

There are two types of Olympic wrestling: freestyle and Greco-Roman. The major difference between the two is that Greco-Roman focuses on the use of upper body strength and restricts **holds** below the waist. The object of both is to score points with holds or to pin your opponent to the mat.

In Greco-Roman wrestling, the athletes use their arms and upper bodies to gain advantage over their opponents.

Martial Arts

Judo is a Japanese **martial art**. Contestants score points during a match. They can also win by pinning their opponent to the mat, forcing them to **submit**, or scoring an **ippon**. Taekwondo is a Korean martial art. Athletes score by landing kicks on their opponent. The first Olympic taekwondo medals were awarded in 2000.

WOW!

Only three boxers have ever won three Olympic gold medals: Teófilo Stevenson and Félix Savón of Cuba, and László Papp of Hungary.

Pulling Punches

Olympic boxers compete in a square "ring." Matches are divided into three three-minute rounds for men and four two-minute rounds for women. A boxer scores points with the five judges by landing punches on his or her opponent. If a boxer loses a match, he or she is out of the tournament.

Olympic boxer Felix Diaz of the Dominican Republic lands a jab punch on his Thai opponent, Manus Boonjumnong.

127

MILITARY SPORTS

The modern pentathlon combines five sports: swimming, running, fencing, **equestrian**, and shooting. The last three of these are known as military sports because they require traditional fighting skills. Archery is another military sport.

Equestrian can be a dangerous sport. Elaine Pen of the Netherlands hangs on as her horse leaps during a cross-country event at the 2012 Olympics.

WOW!

Italian and French fencers have combined to win 89 Olympic gold medals (236 medals total) since 1896.

Super Swords

Fencing showcases athletes who specialize in swordsmanship. Fencers score points by touching parts of their opponents with their sword. The three swords used in Olympic fencing are the épée, foil, and saber. Electrical sensors in the sword tips and the athletes' protective suits tell judges when a touch has been made.

Special equipment protects the fencers and tells judges when one fencer has scored. These fencers are competing with swords called foils.

Horse Riding

Equestrian events involve riders and horses. Dressage is very technical, with the rider and horse precisely performing moves for the judges. In show-jumping, rider and horse leap over obstacles. Eventing combines the two and adds a difficult cross-country event. Pentathletes don't get to "meet" their horse until just before the event.

STAR PROFILE
KIM RHODE

Born: July 16, 1979 Whittier, California

Sport: Shooting (double trap, skeet)

Olympic Record: 3x gold, 1x silver, 1x bronze medalist (1996, 2000, 2004, 2008, 2012)

Taking Aim

Shooting sports have been a part of the modern Olympics since 1896. Today there are several shooting events involving pistols and rifles. Events can vary the position from which the **marksman** shoots. Two of the sports, skeet and trap, require the marksmen to shoot moving targets called clays.

129

SKATING SPORTS

The first Winter Olympics were held in 1924. Athletes at these games compete on the ice and snow. Sports at the Winter Olympics require skis, sleds, and skates!

STAR PROFILE

HAYLEY WICKENHEISER

Born: August 12, 1978 Shaunavon, Saskatchewan, Canada

Sport: Ice hockey

Olympic Record: 18 goals, 33 assists, 4x gold medalist (2002, 2006, 2010, 2014)

Since 1998, the USA and Canada have played in every gold medal game except one. Here is Team USA's Gigi Marvin in the 2014 gold medal game against Canada.

Ice Hockey

The Olympics host ice hockey tournaments for men and women. Twelve teams qualify for each tournament. The Soviet Union dominated Olympic ice hockey from the 1950s through the 1980s. One of the greatest Olympic upsets occurred when the US men's team defeated the Soviets and won the gold medal in 1980's "Miracle on Ice."

Figure Skating

In figure skating, men and women create routines that are rated by judges. The skaters spend countless hours to make sure their routines are flawless. Events include competitions for single skaters and pairs. There's even an ice dancing competition in which the skaters wear costumes, just like ballroom dancers.

Finnish figure skater Laura Lepisto performs at the 2010 World Figure Skating Championship.

Short-track speed skating is one of the most exciting of all Winter Olympic sports.

WOW!

Eric Heiden won five speed skating gold medals at the 1980 Winter Olympics.

Speed Skating

Speed skaters wear special skates with long blades. Like track and swimming, the sport features individual races and team relays. Short races are held on an indoor track, and longer races are held on a bigger outdoor track. Races range in length from 500 to 10,000 meters (547 yards to 6.2 miles).

SKIING

Skiing didn't begin as a sport. Skis were invented as a way to get around more easily on snow. Thousands of years later, Olympic athletes are doing unbelievable things on skis.

Strahinja Stanisic of Serbia turns past a gate during a slalom skiing event. Downhill skiers use poles to help them turn.

WOW!
Olympic downhill skiers hit speeds between 75 and 95 miles per hour!

The Need for Speed

Downhill, or "alpine," skiing involves skiers gliding down mountains at incredible speeds. In downhill and super-G events, skiers aim to get from the start to the finish in the quickest time possible. Skiers in **slalom** events try to reach the finish line in the fastest time, too, but must ski around obstacles called gates.

Cross-Country Courses

Cross-country skiers use thin skis to travel over a course. Like downhill skiers, they have poles to help push themselves along. Races range from 5 to 30 kilometers (3.1 to 18.6 miles) and also include relays. One event, the biathlon, combines cross-country skiing with target shooting.

The biathlon combines cross-country skiing and shooting. Aiming a rifle is a challenge when your heart is pounding after skiing a long distance!

Ski Jumping

Ski jumpers have no poles. They glide down a large ramp on wide skis to see who can travel the farthest distance before touching down on the snow. They are also judged on their form. The ski jump record for distance is 251.5 meters (825 feet)!

Ski jumpers' wide skis are helpful when landing, and also keep skiers in the air longer, like a glider's wing.

ACTION SPORTS

Skiing has a long history, but the Winter Olympics also feature newer sports. Snowboarding and freestyle skiing are two action sports that have been added to the Games in recent decades.

Olympic gold medalist Kelly Clark competes in the Mammoth Grand Prix Half-Pipe Finals in 2010.

Surfing on Snow

Snowboarding was added to the Olympics in 1988. There are five events for both men and women: slalom and giant slalom, half-pipe, slopestyle, and snowboard cross. Slalom is similar to slalom in alpine skiing, with athletes turning around gates. The half-pipe features boarders performing tricks up and down the sides of a U-shaped run.

STAR PROFILE
SHAUN WHITE

Born: September 3, 1986 San Diego, California

Sport: Snowboarding

Olympic Record: 2x gold medalist (2006, 2010)

Canada's Alex Bilodeau skis over the moguls at the 2014 Winter Olympics. Bilodeau won gold medals in the event in both 2010 and 2014.

WOW!

Aerial freestyle skiers reach heights of 55 feet above the spots where they land.

Freestyle Skiing

Freestyle skiing was added to the Olympics in 1992. It features five disciplines: aerial, half-pipe, moguls, ski cross, and slopestyle. In the aerial and half-pipe events skiers do amazing acrobatics. On the moguls, they ski down a hill lined with large bumps, and in ski cross four skiers race against each another, just like in snowboard cross. Slopestyle in both freestyle skiing and snowboarding is inspired by skateboarding—athletes create tricks on **terrain park** features.

Morgan Schild of the USA performs a mogul jump at the 2014 Freestyle Junior World Championships.

SLED SPORTS

Anyone who lives in an area with snowy winters has enjoyed sledding down a neighborhood hill. But how about getting into a sled with your friends and speeding down an iced track at 90 miles per hour? That's exactly what Olympic bobsledders and lugers do!

Bobsleigh

There are three Olympic bobsleigh events: two-man, four-man, and two-woman. The sleigh sits on four steel runners. The crew get a running start and jump one by one into the sleigh. The maximum weight for a four-man bobsleigh with its crew is 1,390 pounds. Each track is different but the usual length is around 4,000 feet.

This is one of Germany's two-man teams at the 2014 Winter Games. Germany has been a leader in the sport.

Adam Rosen of the UK takes part in a men's singles race in Germany in 2015.

WOW!

Although they have yet to win a medal, bobsleigh teams from tropical Jamaica have qualified for six Winter Olympics.

Luge and Skeleton

Like bobsleighers luge athletes speed down an icy track—but without a composite sled body to protect them in a crash. Lugers compete alone or on two-person teams. They lie on their back as they flash down the course feet first. In the skeleton event competitors travel head first!

GLOSSARY

amateur

an athlete who is not paid to play his or her sport; the opposite of professional

apparatus

a piece of equipment that gymnasts use to perform a routine

assist

a point that's awarded to a player who passes the puck or basketball to a teammate who then scores; assists are not recorded on the scoreboard

backboard

the large glass, steel, or wooden board to which a basketball net and hoop are attached

back check

in hockey, to quickly skate back to the defensive zone and help prevent the opponent from scoring

base

one of the spots at the four corners of a baseball diamond; to score, a runner must advance to all four

batter's box

a chalk rectangle on each side of home plate; the batter must stand in one of these

batting average

a baseball player's hits divided by his or her at-bats (minus walks) and carried to the third decimal place

blitz

a football strategy in which linebackers and defensive backs rush the quarterback block in football, using hands and leg strength to prevent a defensive player from reaching the ball carrier

bracket

a diagram that shows the games that are to be played in a tournament

check

in hockey, to knock an opponent away from the puck by hitting them with a shoulder or hip

concussion

a serious head injury caused by hard contact with another player, the ground, ice, or another object

contact sport

a sport that involves contact among players or players and their equipment

drop-kick

to hold a football out in front of the body, drop it, and then kick it; also called a "punt"

dynasty

a team that wins several league championships in a row

ejected

thrown out of a game for arguing with an official, or for breaking another rule

equestrian

sports in which the athletes compete while riding horses

fly ball

a baseball that is hit in a high arc, usually to the outfield

goalpost

one of a pair of tall posts in each end zone through which a football is kicked to score points

grounder

a baseball that rolls along on the ground after it is hit; also called a "ground ball"

handoff

the act of handing a football to a teammate; usually occurs between the quarterback and a running back

hat trick

a feat in hockey or soccer in which one player scores three goals in a single game

hike

the transfer of the football from the center to the quarterback to begin a play

hold

a grip used on an opponent in wrestling to score points or gain another advantage

home plate

the base where a baseball batter stands and which a runner must step on or touch to score

horse

a game in which the winner is the player to make five basketball shots that his or her opponent then misses

GLOSSARY

innings
the nine parts of a baseball game in which teams take turns batting and playing defense

ippon
in judo, throwing an opponent to their back with force

key
the area of a basketball court from the end line beneath the net to the free-throw line; also called the "lane" and the "paint"

huddle
the grouping together of a football team's offense before a play to discuss strategy

infield
the area of a baseball field that includes the bases and the pitcher's mound

kickoff
a play in which the football is kicked from one team to the other to begin the game

line drive
a baseball that is hit hard and in a straight line without touching the ground

line of scrimmage
the imaginary line across a football field on which a ball is set before a play

marksman
an athlete who competes in sports to see who is the best target shooter with a pistol or a firearm

martial art
a combat sport, usually from Asia, that is practiced for self-defense, competition, or exercise

mixed doubles
teams of two in racket sports that include one female and one male athlete

neutral site
a stadium that is not in the home city of either team playing in the game

no-hitter
a performance in which a pitcher plays all nine innings and allows zero hits

140

one-on-one

informal game in which two basketball players compete against each other, usually on a half-court

outfield

the large grassy area of a baseball field that is located past the infield

physical education

the teaching of exercise, sports, and healthy habits; sometimes simply called "phys ed"

pickup

describes an informal game in which players show up and sides are chosen

playbook

a thick book that contains diagrams of all the plays a football team uses

postseason

the playoffs that occur after a sport's leagues' regular season

rebound

in basketball, the recovery of a missed shot that bounces off the backboard or rim

roster

a list of the members of a sports team

rounders

a game similar to baseball that originated in England in the 1500s

routine

a performance that gymnasts plan and practice for competition

rushing

advancing the football up the field by carrying it

sack

the tackling of the quarterback by a defensive player behind the line of scrimmage

save

in baseball, a performance by a relief pitcher that helps his or her team win the game

shuttlecock

the cone-shaped object hit over a badminton net and made of a small cork ball with plastic "feathers" attached; also called a "birdie"

sideline

the line marking the edge of one long side of a football field

slalom

a downhill ski competition in which skiers must make alternate turns around flags called "gates"

slam dunk

the jamming of a basketball through the rim

GLOSSARY

slap shot

hitting a puck sharply with the stick to send it toward the opponent's net at great speed

slot

the area right in front of the hockey goal crease

special teams

the offensive and defensive units that are on the field for any sort of kicking play

stats

numbers used in any sport to measure an athlete's performance

steal

a stolen base, which occurs when a runner advances one base without the aid of a hit or walk by a teammate

steroids

certain types of drugs that can increase an athlete's performance

stickhandle

to control a puck by dribbling it back and forth with the blade of a hockey stick

strike

a baseball pitch at which a batter swings but misses, or that passes through the strike zone without the batter swinging

stroke

a method of swimming used to move through the water; the four strokes used in Olympic swimming are freestyle, backstroke, butterfly, and breaststroke

sub

a player sent into a game to relieve a tired teammate or to better match up against an opponent

submit

in a combat sport, to admit that your opponent has gained the upper hand and won the match

tackle

in football, using arms or hands to pull the opponent carrying the ball to the ground

terrain park

an area with features such as stairs and railings used for skiing, snowboarding, and skateboarding competitions

tread water

to stay in one place and upright in deep water by moving the legs and hands in a circular motion

walk

a pass to first base given to a baseball batter when he or she receives four pitches outside the strike zone

wild card

a team that's awarded a playoff spot despite not winning its division in the regular season

INDEX